You Deserve More:

A Single Woman's Guide to Marriage

TO: Carla Burch,

How to Select and Invest in a Lifetime Partner

*You Deserve More... Know it...
Demand it!*

Dr. Dwayne L. Buckingham

Dwayne L. Buckingham,

Ph.D., LCSW, BCD

Other Great Books by Dr. Dwayne L. Buckingham

Resilient Thinking: The Power of Embracing Realistic and Optimistic Thoughts about Life, Love and Relationships

Can Black Women Achieve Marital Satisfaction? How Childhood Nurturing Experiences Impact Marital Happiness

Unconditional Love: What Every Woman and Man Desire in a Relationship

A Black Man's Worth: Conqueror and Head of Household

A Black Woman's Worth: My Queen and Backbone

Groundbreaking Films by Dr. Dwayne L. Buckingham

A Black Man's Worth: Conqueror and Head of Household

A Black Woman's Worth: My Queen and Backbone

Qualified, yet Single: Why Good Men Remain Single

www.drbuckingham.com

You Deserve More:

A Single Woman's Guide to Marriage

How to Select and Invest in a Lifetime Partner

Dwayne L. Buckingham, Ph.D., LCSW, BCD

An Imprint of RHCS Publishing

You Deserve More: A Single Woman's Guide to Marriage
Copyright © 2015 by Dr. Dwayne L. Buckingham

To protect the confidentially and privacy of individuals who have shared their stories, identifiable information has been modified.

To order additional copies of this book or to place bulk orders, please visit www.realhorizonsdlb.com or write to:

R.E.A.L. Horizons Consulting Service, LLC
P.O. Box 2665
Silver Spring, MD 20915
240-242-4087 Voice mail
www.drbuckingham.com

FIRST EDITION
Design by Visual Arts
Library of Congress Control Number: 2014960129
ISBN: 978-0-9855765-6-1
Edited by Lauren Westy
For Worldwide Distribution
Printed in the United States of America

Dedication

To every single woman who desires marriage
but struggles to find a lifetime partner

Message to Marriage-Minded Women

You are worthy of receiving whatever your heart desires,
but remember that a man can only treat you badly or
disrespectfully if you allow him to do so. Time after time,
some of you complain about how some men are no good
and are preoccupied with conquering women. As you reflect
on your view of men, commitment and relationships, stop to
ask yourself if you are a good judge of character. The
easiest way to judge the men you choose to interact with is
to look at yourself. Do you possess qualities that are
required to be married? Are you truly ready for marriage?
Do you have any unresolved emotional shortcomings? As
you take this educational journey with me, I encourage you
to look at yourself. Remember that entering into and
sustaining a healthy marriage is only possible if two people
are willing to reflect on and address their own emotional
shortcomings.

Message to Single Women Who Play Games

Stop playing games and making it difficult for marriage-
minded single women who truly desire lifetime
commitment. Do not engage and deceive men if you have
no intention of doing right by us. Game playing is
counterproductive to God's Divine plan for man and
woman. He created man and woman to honor and
compliment each other, not to dishonor and play each other.

Fear

If you are attractive, I will tell you what you want to hear
But please do not listen too close because you might hear
my fear.

Leading you on is not difficult to do
Because you are like a broken table and I am the glue.

I shine on the outside so you can't see through
But underneath the façade my heart is cold and blue.

You think I am the one so you don't mind the wait
And have convinced yourself to believe that what we have
is fate.

I tell you I want to be with you because you are great
Open up your eyes, woman, most men use the same bait.

I have great qualifications that you might like,
But everything that looks good on the outside is not right.

I tell you I care, but will not let you near
But you continue to hold on like I am some kind of
souvenir.

If you want to find true love, pay attention to what you hear
Because "good" men like myself will not commit to
marriage until we conquer our fear.

Take Home Messages:

Good to You does not mean Good for You!
Look Beyond the Surface!

Acknowledgments

I would like to acknowledge and thank all the men who provided insight and shared their personal views and stories about commitment, women and marriage.

To my sisters, Linda, Alma, Cynthia and Bonnie, for helping me develop the fortitude to treat women with respect and dignity as I ventured into marriage.

To my Godmother, Eugenia, I am appreciative of the ongoing support you provide in my quest to understand and do right by women.

To my dear friends, LaNetra Kellar and Jennifer Jones, who spent numerous hours and days talking to me about women and challenged me to explore and process my fear as a single man. Our conversations ignited a flame in me that served as the foundation for finding my lifetime partner and writing this book.

To marriage-minded women all around the world, you all have not given up on sanctified love despite the emotional and physical challenges you all face at the hands of men on a daily basis. I truly appreciate the strength and courage you all display in putting your hearts on the line.

Thanks for encouraging me to do right; I am truly sorry for any despair you experience on your quest to find a lifetime partner.

Glossary of Terms

Qualifications: Qualities that make single men suitable for marriage. These include: financial stability, responsibility, ambition, success and being family oriented.

Qualified Men: Men who possess certain personal and/or professional attributes that women find attractive and appealing.

Good Men: Men who are desirable by nature because they are kind, thoughtful, easy going, good spirited, honest, giving and considerate.

A Jump-Off: A woman who gives of herself sexually without wanting much in return. She is easily persuaded and impressed with a man's outwardly appearance, status and verbal presentation.

Emotionally-Unavailable Men: Men who do not share their inner feelings, thoughts or desires. They desire and seek companionship, but do not invest emotionally.

Fear: A debilitating and anxiety-provoking emotion that triggers a fight-or-flight response.

Contents

Preface

~

Knowledge Is the Equalizer

As you read this book, keep an open mind and heart. I make generalizations about single men throughout the book, but remember that every man is unique in his own right. I did not write this book so that you can condemn, belittle or denigrate single men. I wrote it to empower you and to help you do a better job of selecting men who have the potential to be lifetime partners.

In thinking about the pain that millions of marriage-minded single women have endured at the hands of single good men, I felt a strong need to provide you with information that will help you make healthier and more informed choices about selecting and investing in a lifetime partner.

On a regular basis, I am asked, "How do I deal with a single good man who is not truly interested in making me a lifetime partner?" My reply: "Acquire knowledge about single good men—their psychological makeup, behavior and mode of operation."

Without proper knowledge, your ability to understand and deal with single good men will not evolve. How often do you equip yourself with information that will help you solve or cope with the difficulties of interacting with single good men who do not commit? There are some things in life in which you can excel through experimentation and practice alone; however, selecting and investing in a lifetime partner is not one of them.

Can you imagine what your relationship would be like if you secured knowledge about men from the perspective of an experienced and competent man and combined it with your intuition?

Empower yourself by acquiring knowledge and applying it. *Remember that acquisition of knowledge is not power; application of knowledge is power.* Lack of understanding and knowledge are the root causes of most conflict between women and men. Do not continue to struggle unnecessarily. This book will enhance your ability to select and invest in a lifetime partner—remember that knowledge is the equalizer.

Yours Truthfully,

Dwayne L. Buckingham, Ph.D., LCSW, BCD

Introduction

You Deserve More:
Look Beyond the Surface

Since I am known for being a straightforward and honest man, I usually do not bite my tongue when it comes to expressing my thoughts about single women who are sacrificing their minds and bodies outside of matrimony. So here it is–*You Deserve More*.

According to Hebrews 13:4, marriage is honourable in all, and the bed undefiled; but whoremongers and adulterers, God will judge. As God's most valuable gift to man, you deserve to be placed on a pedestal and treated like a priceless diamond. Given this, you should strive passionately to be with a man who is thriving mentally, spiritually and financially. Do not settle for a man who cannot stimulate you mentally through intelligent conversation, uplift you spiritually by faith and support you financially by maintaining employment. Bond with a man who is sensitive enough or interested in understanding what you go through as a woman, and who will strive to keep you grounded. You need a man you can respect. And I encourage you to be submissive, but only if you respect him. Do not submit to a man who does not take care of his business; please stop investing your time. Give yourself to a God-fearing man who is worthy of having you and will honor God and you by making you his wife.

One of the greatest injustices that you face as a single woman is trying to obtain lifetime commitment while receiving empty words from the man that you love. Unfortunately, thousands of single women like you are selecting and investing in men who have no intentions of marrying them. If you desire to be married, be patient and respect yourself. Do not chase any man. Allow your king to find you. A man who understands your worth and strives to comply with God's *Word*, will find and pursue you. God rewards all who abide by his *Word.* Proverbs 18:22 informs all men, especially Christian men, that God will reward them for finding you: "He who finds a wife finds what is good and receives favor from the Lord." With this in mind, you should expect a lot because you are worthy of a lot.

God created man and woman to complete each other, and He designed the institution of marriage so that we could live happily ever after. Marriage is a time when two lives join together and become one family unit. Marriage is a time when a man accepts full responsibility for you and affords you all the rights that comes with fidelity. Marriage is a time when you commit and remain devoted until death. Marriage is a time when man and woman show respect for God's design – "then the Lord said, 'It is not good that man should be alone; I will make him a helper fit for him" (Genesis 2:18).

Although marriage is honorable in the eyes of God, millions of single women have given up on sanctified love. *Why?* I personally believe that many of you have given up on sanctified love because you have been persuaded to believe that *men are simple.* This simplistic kind of reasoning has and will continue to create hardships for you as you journey toward marriage.

While it is true that a large percentage of men engage in similar behavior, I do not believe that our behavior can be fully understood by taking us for face value. As a licensed and experienced psychotherapist, my thoughts regarding men and our behavior go beyond the surface views most men and women discuss on radio shows and in barber and beauty shops throughout America. I say this not to offend anyone or to minimize their opinions, but to basically emphasize that human behavior and development are very complicated topics. Personal views, including mine, should be taken with a grain of salt. I encourage you to study and do your own research about men.

Men are like gold. We shine on the outside, but in our rawest form, we are usually dull. I use this analogy to say that men are too complex to be taken at surface value. I have three degrees in human behavior and development and have provided individual and marital therapy to more than thirty thousand women and men over the past sixteen years—and I, like you, still get frustrated trying to understand the differences between women and men.

Understanding how men think, feel and act in relationships is not an easy task; there are a multitude of theories and explanations that attempt to provide insight into this phenomenon. Again, I encourage you to study, but remember that there is no one "right" theory or explanation. Therefore, use what works for you and let the rest go. I do not claim to have all the answers about men's thoughts or behaviors, but I can tell you that men are not simple. If that were the case, this book and other relationship books would not exist.

Most women, especially single good women like yourself, have been taught to select men who possess qualities that are compatible with yours. While this is good advice, have you ever thought about why so many single "good" men attract and entice women without committing? Have you ever stopped to think about what most single "good" men have in common that makes them desirable? Please allow me to enlighten you.

We live in a society that places a great deal of emphasis on outward appearance, title and status. Unfortunately, many of us take things at face value. I am guilty of this as well. However, as a result of interacting with thousands of women and men with various life problems, *I have learned that behind every behavior there is an emotional or psychological issue associated with it.*

For example, men who are focused on succeeding and work extremely hard could potentially be suffering from low self-esteem or insecurity. They may work hard because they feel that they have to prove themselves to others. Many people would say that there is nothing wrong with working hard— some men just have good work ethics. Sounds simple, right? I am not implying that all men who work hard are "screwed up or suffer from low self-esteem," but whatever their reasons are for working hard, there are emotions associated with them. This is difficult for most women to identify and understand because most of you do not think to ask or don't care enough to explore the cause of men's behavior, especially if the behavior is good in nature. If a man possesses good qualities or attributes and is desirable, some of you might say, "Who cares if he works hard because he has low self-esteem or feels insecure, as long as he brings the money home?"

For the women who care: what would you do if you met a man who was financially stable, presented well and treated you like a queen, but would not marry you? This is a difficult question that many of you struggle with on a daily basis. The answer is not simple because there are plenty of men who shine on the outside, but struggle emotionally or psychologically. I know a lot of good men who are attractive, competent, reliable, genuine, enjoyable, kind, ambitious, successful and honorable, but who have no intention of getting married. I socialize with men who attract women simply based on how they look. However, there are other men I socialize with who take care of business. They take care of their personal responsibilities and are progressing professionally as single men. And before they approach you, they make sure that you cannot identify their emotional or psychological shortcomings too easily. Hiding their emotional shortcomings from you is not difficult because many of you do not know what to look for. Some of you might wonder and ask yourself, "What's wrong with this man? Why is he still single?" but will not follow through with your curiosity because you are impressed with his physical and/or intellectual presentation.

Prior to finding my wife, I was once one of those single "good" men who impressed women with my physical and intellectual presentation. Keeping my body and mind fit allowed me to pass without committing. Even though I was more than prepared for marriage from a social status and financial perspective, I was not convinced that marriage was honorable. For many years I toyed with women and never seriously considered marriage.

Here is why:

As a child I lacked an understanding about the institution of marriage because no man ever taught me the importance of respecting, honoring or marrying a woman. Most of the women in my life had children out of wedlock, and as a result, I grew up viewing all women negatively and believed that they were not worthy of marriage. I thought women were weak because they did things that nobody else would do and loved men who did not love them or commit to them. My mother birthed eight children and practically raised us by herself. She instilled the fear of God in us and taught us to be generous, but she was not married. I remember having mixed feeling about my mother as a child.

I loved her wholeheartedly for taking care of me, but I was also angry with her. My siblings and I were often teased about not having a father present. I felt embarrassed and wondered why my mother was not married when I was born. She married one of my older siblings' fathers, but gave up on sanctified love afterward. I never discussed the embarrassment or disappointment with my mother prior to her death, and as a result, I never understood why she gave up on sanctified love.

As I ventured toward manhood, my view of marriage did not improve much. Witnessing the hardships and pain of my four sisters compounded my ambivalence and negativity about single women and marriage. My sisters had children at early ages and engaged in activities similar to those of my mother: up-and-down relationships and raising their children alone. Only one of my sisters married, but her marriage only lasted a few years because she married a "good" man who was not husband material.

Growing up and observing the hardships experienced by the women I cherished and loved was emotionally devastating. However, due to a lack of knowledge and respectable male role models, I grew up treating females the same way I saw men treat my mother and sisters. Love them and leave them. That is what I was used to.

By now, I hope you understand why you have to look beyond the surface. Single "good" men are difficult to understand—some of them are willing to love and commit to you, but may struggle with unresolved emotional or psychological issues. Before single "good" men can give you what you deserve—marriage—they must first resolve their own emotional or psychological issues. I did!

As a result of seeking suitable counsel, which enabled me to acquire proper knowledge and wisdom about women and marriage, I transformed from a lost, disturbed, disrespectful, unappreciative *child* to a thoughtful, caring, spiritual and generous *man* who now respects, honors and appreciates my wife. "When I was a child, I spoke as a child, I understood as a child, I thought as a child; but when I became a man, I put away childish things" (1 Corinthians 13:11).

I thank God for my transformation and lifetime partner. And because I want you to be transformed and blessed with a lifetime partner, I have taken it upon myself to be your personal psychotherapist and relationship coach.

You Deserve More: A Single Woman's Guide to Marriage is dedicated to all the single women like you, who deserve more than what you are settling for. If you desire to be married it is imperative that you dig a little deeper—look beyond men's surface or outward appearance.

In its most fundamental sense, *You Deserve More: A Single Woman's Guide to Marriage* is an investment guide for marriage-minded single women who are tired of wasting their time on single "good" men who struggle with formal commitment. Men's emotional problems should not be your responsibility to fix. Demand that they resolve their own emotional shortcomings with or without you. No more excuses. This book offers a wealth of information that is based on more than seventeen years of personal experience as a single man, upwards of sixteen years of clinical experience as a relationship expert, and nine years of advanced academic instruction.

Now that you have decided that you would *like to* invest in a lifetime partner, I will teach you *how* to invest. If you are enticed or deceived by single "good" men who are not ready for marriage, don't blame them. I hope that this book inspires you to think more deeply about your potential lifetime partner and to realize that good to you does not mean good *for* you.

Any time you invest in a man, you are devoting your heart, time, resources and efforts to achieve a greater goal. You should only invest your time in a relationship if you believe that it will prosper over time. Remember: *You Deserve More: A Single Woman's Guide to Marriage* is your reminder that "all that glitters is not gold." Behind every behavior there is an emotion and motive. Select wisely and invest properly and you will get what you deserve: lifetime commitment.

Part One

The Selection Process:
Great Candidate, but Not a
Lifetime Partner

Chapter 1

The Psychological Trap:
Fear, Fixation and Firmness

One of the most challenging aspects of getting what you deserve is your inability to distinguish single "good" men who are great candidates from those who are potential lifetime partners. As you improve your marriage selection skills and learn to look beyond a man's surface, you will understand that most single "good" men have the desire to settle down with the women of their dreams, buy the big white house in the suburbs and contribute to the birth of one and a half kids. However, a large percentage of single men do not take that ultimate step toward oneness with that special woman because they are enslaved by fear, fixation and firmness. These three emotions typically dominate single "good" men and often dictate how they behave. If you do not learn anything else about single good men from this book, understand that fear, fixation and firmness are emotions that are deeply embedded in their psyche and often prevent many of them from entering into marriage. Stop wasting your time listening to men run "game" and start paying attention to their emotional makeup.

No matter how qualified a man may be—he will not marry you until he has successfully conquered his fear, eliminated his fixation and minimized his firmness. The more fear a man experiences, the more fixated he will become, and his increased fixation will contribute to intense firmness. I refer to this as the Fear-Fixation-Firmness Cycle. And guess what? You are the trigger that sets this cycle in motion. Let me enlighten you about this emotionally debilitating cycle that enslaves most single "good" men.

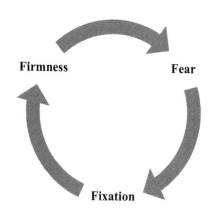

Firmness   **Fear**

Fixation

Fear

Fear is a distressing emotion that manifests psychologically when a man perceives that his well-being, identity, emotional stability or freedom is being or will be threatened. The loss of control or the threat of pain is often associated with fear. You may hear men say that they do not enter committed relationships because they are afraid of having one sex partner for the rest of their lives, afraid of being taken advantage of or afraid of losing their freedom. While all of these things do create fear in men, I personally believe that the fear of falling in love or being emotionally vulnerable is what truly inhibits single good men from committing.

Falling in love or being emotionally vulnerable creates anxiety for men because it is associated with losing control, feeling weak and experiencing pain. In general, vulnerability is perceived to be very negative by most men. After years of reflecting on my relationship patterns, I realized that I would always find reasons to discredit and chase good women away because of my fear. Whenever I would start developing feelings for a woman I would experience this intense form of anxiety that often demobilized me. And the more I experienced fear, the more I pushed women away.

In the midst of my anxiety-provoking crisis years, I had difficulty entering and sustaining relationships with women without attempting to establish some emotional controls and boundaries. When dating, I made sure that women knew that I was not going to take them seriously. Looking back on my behavior, I now understand that I detached myself from women because I feared being vulnerable. The thought of being vulnerable and allowing myself the potential to be hurt by a woman intensified my fear. If I experienced any distress or felt fearful as a result of something a woman said or did, I moved quickly to protect myself—I cut her off.

For many years, I did not understand why I reacted so strongly whenever I felt fearful, like I was losing control, or emotionally vulnerable. Year after year, I would find myself engaging in the same defensive behavior and would do whatever was needed to keep women at a distance. I realized that this behavior was not healthy for me, but I was in control of my emotions.

There were times during my mid-twenties when I longed for and desperately wanted to love and be loved by that special woman, but my fear would not allow me to lower my guard or remove my emotional armor. The desire to have companionship consumed me daily, but fear of being hurt and vulnerable had more of an emotional hold on me. Despite any efforts I made to accommodate or cater to women, I knew in my heart that I would not allow a woman to enter my life until I understood and conquered my fear.

Understanding and conquering my fear was not an easy task. How often do you hear men talk about their fear? Probably not too often because we typically do not discuss our emotions, especially emotions that make us look weak. It is not cool in some quarters to be viewed as weak when interacting with women, so most of us do not disclose how we truly feel. We have been taught that men should not show fear or vulnerability. Fear is perceived by the majority of men as some minor emotion that should be ignored or met with aggression. Given this stereotypical mindset, I would not disclose my fear and if I did share, I felt that women did not connect with me because they perceived me as being either too arrogant or aggressive.

Date after date, I found myself feeling empty as I struggled with the fact that I could enjoy women's physical company, but would not allow myself to give in or connect with them emotionally. As with most men, I suppressed how I really felt and began my journey toward understanding and conquering my fear in solitude and silence. Attempting to understand the source of my fear consumed me emotionally for many years.

Then, one night while lying in bed I began to think deeply about all my past relationships and processed how each one impacted my behavior and perceptions of women. After playing each relationship over and over in my head, there was one that stood out and caused me to feel anxious instantly. I'll never forget the fear, pain and vulnerability that I experienced after going through a difficult and upsetting break-up while in college. Reflecting on my college dating experience helped me understand the source of my fear.

During my sophomore year in college, I met an attractive young woman named Monica. Initially, I had no intention of dating or being serious with Monica because she was nine-months pregnant. But as we interacted, I felt some emotional and physical chemistry develop, so I inquired about her situation and relationship status. Monica informed me that she had gotten pregnant with a guy she dated for a short period, but was no longer with him because he left her after she got pregnant. I did not think much about her situation; after all, I was not looking to start a serious relationship.

Monica was a southwestern girl who had a good spirit and always appeared to be happy. Her positive spirit was intoxicating so I began to flirt with her and we decided to hang out. Shortly after we started hanging out, Monica delivered her daughter, Jessica. At first, I was not too concerned about being involved with a young female who had just delivered a child, because my "other head" was dictating most of my decisions and moves at that point in my life.

After Monica gave birth to Jessica, our interactions increased and I began to look forward to hanging out with her during the weekends at her mother's house. The very first day that I visited, Monica's ex-boyfriend called and threatened to come over because she told him she had company. Monica mentioned this to me, but I was not concerned because I did not know the fellow; he never showed up.

In the coming months Monica and I spent a great deal of time together and she decided to get her own apartment. I spent nights at her place and we enjoyed each other's company. I was skating on cloud nine and thought I was doing it "big" because I had a female who had her own place and was willing to feed me and have sex with me any time.

During the earlier stage of the relationship, Monica would take her daughter to her mother's house so that her ex-boyfriend could pick her up from there. This was fine with me because I did not feel a need to meet the guy, especially since I thought he was a bum for leaving his woman while she was pregnant. We never talked about her ex-boyfriend, so I did not know much about him. Monica did not feel the need to tell me anything about him and I did not feel the need to ask. I guess we were in love and did not want to say or do anything that would damage our relationship. At that point in my life, I did not know what love meant, but I felt something close it. We were living a peaceful fairytale relationship.

Monica and I kicked it for approximately nine months before our fairytale relationship changed. As time passed, she got tired of dropping her daughter off at her mother's house, so she decided to tell her ex-boyfriend where she lived so he could pick their daughter up from the apartment. This single decision significantly impacted our relationship and we never recovered.

July 12, 1994 was the day I learned what it feels like to experience the loss of control in a relationship. I also learned about the pain that is associated with being emotionally vulnerable. On this particular day, Monica's ex-boyfriend came to pick up their daughter. As he entered the apartment around 4:30 p.m., I was sitting on the couch watching football. He introduced himself and asked who was playing. I introduced myself and mentioned the names of the two football teams. He gathered Jessica's belongings and left with her. Shortly after he left, the phone rang and I heard Monica raise her voice. Within 30 minutes of the phone call, her ex-boyfriend returned and dropped Jessica back off.

I inquired about what was going on and Monica told me that her ex-boyfriend was mad because she had another man around his daughter. I asked if I needed to leave and Monica said, "No, everything is okay." We went on with our day and got in bed around midnight. At approximately 2 a.m. in the morning, I was awakened by loud kicking and knocking at the front door. Monica jumped out of bed and rushed to the door because she did not want the noise to wake up Jessica. I could hear Monica's ex-boyfriend say, "Let me in to see my daughter. I am going back to California in the morning and I want to see my daughter." After he finished yelling and cursing, I heard Monica say, "You have been drinking. Leave or I will call the police." At this point, I decided to get out of bed so I could check on Monica. As I rolled out of bed, I heard Monica say, "Don't push me," and then I heard the door hit the wall. I quickly put on my shorts and attempted to stand up, but before I could stand-up completely, Monica's ex-boyfriend grabbed me. We tossed and turned until we ended up in the living room. He attempted to hit me and I attempted to hit him.

Monica was crying and screaming, "You better leave my apartment now or I will call the police." She ran to the bedroom and grabbed her gun and the telephone. By the time she entered the living room, we had stopped wrestling. Monica told her ex-boyfriend to leave, but he refused. She handed me the gun and called the police.

The police arrived and asked me if I wanted to press charges for assault and battery. I told the police that I didn't want to press charges because I felt that I could address the issue without getting the judicial system involved. The police encouraged me to file a report in case something bad happened in the future. With a hostile look on my face, I replied, "I can take care of it myself. I am not worried about having anything on file." They took the handcuffs off Monica's ex-boyfriend and allowed him to leave.

To make a long story short, I spent the next few months on an emotional rollercoaster. Monica's ex-boyfriend threatened me often and occasionally showed up at my job. As a result I started carrying a gun to work daily and eventually decided to quit my job because I did not want anything to happen to innocent people.

In an attempt to support me and protect herself, Monica got a restraining order against her ex-boyfriend. I was glad that Monica was looking out for me, but the drama was taking a toll on me emotionally. Nevertheless, I decided to hang in there with Monica for a few more months because I felt I was in love. The love thing was new to me so I did not know how to deal with pain that sometimes accompanies love. I did not know that loving someone could be so dramatic and painful. This was all new to me and I had never felt so vulnerable and out of control before.

After having frequent intense encounters with Monica's ex-boyfriend, I decided to call it quits. I told Monica that I felt that it would be best for everyone if I just moved on with my life. She was devastated, but understood. We both felt hurt and defeated. Walking away was emotionally devastating for me, but I knew that I could not remain in the relationship any longer. We decided to remain friends and I told Monica that I would check on her from time to time.

Several weeks passed before I decided to call to check on Monica. I had mixed feelings about calling because I still had strong feelings for her. Nevertheless, I decided to call one Saturday morning to check on her. When she answered the phone she appeared to be distant with me. I was somewhat bothered and hurt because that was not Monica's normal way of acting. Confused and concerned, I decided to stop by her apartment. When she answered the door and saw me, her faced dropped. Monica looked like she had just seen a ghost. I asked her what was wrong and she said she did not want any trouble. As I entered the apartment, I saw her daughter crawling by the bedroom door. I immediately, thought, "Why is the baby in the back of the apartment alone?"

I began to walk down the hall and Monica shouted, "I don't want any trouble." As I opened the door her ex-boyfriend was lying across the bed with no clothes on. My heart dropped immediately and I thought, "I should attack him, like he attacked me." But despite how I felt, I decided to leave. I left the apartment immediately and drove around for approximately 30 minutes to gather myself. I was not in a good place emotionally. One side of my mind was telling me to go back to the apartment and shoot him and the other side was telling me to let it go.

Disturbed and confused, I returned to the apartment with a gun in my pocket. I knocked on the door and told Monica that I wanted to talk to her and her ex-boyfriend. She begged me not to start any trouble if she allowed me to come in. I promised not to start any trouble so she opened the door. As she opened the door she started crying and apologizing. She could see the hurt and pain in my eyes. I did not say anything to her. I approached her ex-boyfriend and sat across from him on the couch. I stared at him with my hand in my pocket. He was not sure how to respond to me because he could see the anger in my eyes, and he did not know what was in my pocket.

I took a deep breath and started talking. I told him that he better do right by Monica because he put me through so much just to get her back. He looked at me and said, "I know she is a good woman and I plan to do right this time." I asked him to leave the living room so that Monica and I could talk alone. I asked Monica why she decided to get back with her ex-boyfriend after all the drama he had put us through. Monica replied, "I did not feel that any other man would deal with the drama that you dealt with. Also, I felt trapped because he is the father of my daughter." I understood what Monica was saying on an intellectual level, but I was still filled with hurt and anger. I walked out of Monica's apartment that day in pain and vulnerability. *As I drove out of the apartment complex, I vowed that I would never allow myself to feel that way again.* I never spoke to

Monica again, but heard that she had eventually married her ex-boyfriend.

With a multitude of women on campus, I quickly put the experience behind me and started hanging out with other young women. I spent my last year in college having sex with a few different women and kicking it with my fraternity brothers. I told females upfront that I was only interested in having sex and fun. Women accepted my position and my remaining days in college were filled with fraternity parties and sex with a multitude of young women who were not interested in having a serious relationship.

The emotional, "I want to be in love" young man had disappeared and so did my desire to be in a committed relationship. I finished my undergraduate degree and enrolled in graduate school at Michigan State University a year later. I started a new chapter in my life, but my perception about committed relationships and interaction with women did not change.

The reason I share my story is to help you understand that *behind every behavior there is an emotion*. Please understand that men do not act up without having a reason. Some men may lack insight and give simple reasons for their behavior, but believe me: whatever their reason is for their behavior, there is an underlying emotion associated with it. I am here to tell you that educated, successful, confident, ambitious and highly-respected men are typically the ones who have the most difficulty understanding and conquering their fear. I say this because my fear intensified as I achieved success. I did not feel comfortable discussing or sharing my fear with women who perceived me to be the "total" package. Women frequently placed me on a pedestal and often asked, "Why are you still single?" Like most single "good" men, I usually responded by saying, "I can't find a good woman," "I am focusing on my career," "I am finishing school" or "I am too picky." But deep down inside I wanted to say, "I am scared."

For a long time I did not disclose my fear to anyone, especially women, because most women were more impressed with the initials behind my name. They did not truly care to understand my emotional temperament. So, despite my underlying fear and unwillingness to commit, I did not have a problem attracting women and keeping them in hands' reach, just in case I felt a need to be entertained or pleasured sexually. To be truthful, keeping women in hands' reach for pleasure and entertainment purposes became much easier as I enhanced my money-making potential.

Similar to most single, successful and ambitious men, I quickly learned that a large percentage of women would tolerate nonsense and wait around for a man who is perceived to be a great candidate, especially if he has a decent financial portfolio and presents well. As I dated, I realized that my charming, considerate and respectful qualities, along with my financial stability, placed me in a position to dictate the nature and frequency of my interactions with women. Some women liked the fact that I was stern and confident, so I got away with dealing with them on my terms.

Most single good men understand that women are impressed by men who present themselves as strong and fearless, so it is not difficult to convince them to fall into place. If a man can manipulate and dominate a woman while masking his fear, he will do exactly that. We will typically do whatever is needed to avoid being hurt or feeling too vulnerable.

Understand that fear is an anxiety-provoking emotion that drives single good men into self-preservation mode. Pay attention to our reactions when we feel threatened. You will notice that most of us say or do things that are intended to protect and preserve ourselves. And although this self-preservation behavior is natural for men and women who feel fearful, men often do not address their fear head on, especially in relationships.

No matter how confident a man may appear on the outside, he will not be able to offer you emotional security, love or lifetime commitment if he has not conquered his fear. In fact, unconquered fear will cause him to suffer from fixation and will definitely keep the *Fear-Fixation-Firmness Cycle* in full rotation.

Fixation

Fixation has to do with a man's state of mind and is best defined as an unhealthy and compulsive preoccupation with something or someone. The most debilitating component of fixation is obsession, which refers to a fixed idea or unwanted emotion that is associated with fear. You probably know men who have one-track minds. Their minds are completely obsessed with a single thought or idea and they rarely entertain alternative viewpoints.

Men who experience fixation typically express it through their stories. For example, whenever a woman inquired about my past relationships, I always mentioned the relationship that I had during my sophomore year in college. It never failed; time after time I shared that experience with every woman who asked me about my previous relationships. The more I thought about it, the more I realized that single relationship played a major factor in how I interacted with and treated women. The loss of control and vulnerability I felt during my college puppy-love experience was deeply embedded in my psyche. I played that painful experience over and over in my mind as I ventured into manhood and began to date other women. This is what fixation truly means. My mind was often preoccupied with that experience and no matter how much I cared about a woman, I always thought about the hurt and pain I endured while dating in college. That experience caused me to become obsessed with avoiding painful and vulnerable emotions. My fixation with pain and not feeling vulnerable led to an emotional coldness that surfaced when women attempted to strip me of my emotional armor.

When a man is in full fixation mode, his inflexibility and firmness will prevent you from breaking down or stripping him of his emotional armor. Just think about it: if you were afraid of something or did not have adequate skills to cope, you would likely rely on skills you developed from previous experiences to protect yourself. This is what men do. We fixate and then become firm because we are afraid. Unresolved fixation will keep the Fear-Fixation-Firmness cycle in rotation because most men will become inflexible and firm—"no means no." Firmness is displayed to prevent potentially painful or vulnerable experiences from recurring.

Firmness

The ability to control and safeguard one's emotions in relationships drives most single good men. And anything or anybody who poses a threat will be met with resistance or hostility. Firmness is an emotional reaction that often surfaces in men when thoughts of pain arise. Once a man perceives that he will lose control, his firmness or unwillingness to compromise will intensify. And he will say and do whatever is needed to maintain control of the situation. Unfortunately, as his fear intensifies, so will his firmness.

You have probably noticed that a lot of men struggle with compromise, especially if they perceive that they will be left feeling vulnerable. Demonstrating firmness is our way of saying, "I'm in control." During this period, you will not be able to reason with us because we are most likely reacting to our fear. When fear is present or perceived, our reactions are more instinctive in nature—protect or destroy. Verbal attacks, stubbornness or irrational behavior will likely occur when we are locked into "firm" man mode. Firmness is a coping or adapting technique that we use to safeguard ourselves and to prevent fear and pain from impacting and dominating us. Men will show firmness in many ways. For me, firmness was illustrated through my unwillingness to date women with children. From my heartbreaking college experience, I learned that some women who have baby daddies are not in positions to freely negotiate how they want to live their lives. As long as their baby's father is involved or paying child support, he will always have the right to be a part of his child's life, and in some ways he can also impact the child's mother. With this in mind, I became adamant about not dating women with children. And although I realized that Monica's boyfriend was crazy, my fear and fixation regarding the experience intensified my firmness.

See, women, this is what unconquered fear does to a number of men, even single good men. It sets unreasonable thinking into play and some of us become very firm in our thinking and doing, even if it is irrational. Sometimes we will argue and even start fights just to show you that we have the ability to control or dominate situations. Sounds terrible and immature, right? It is, but men will frequently respond in a firm manner whenever we are upset or afraid. Many of us have not been taught to express ourselves assertively. Being aggressive and putting our foot down occasionally is a rite of passage that every man believes he has earned. I personally believe it is okay to be firm, but men who respond in a firm manner out of fear should be called on the carpet.

Men are not very courageous when it comes to addressing and dealing with emotions, especially fear. Most of us are scared. Emotions do not have a reasoning component associated with them; therefore, men struggle with understanding the feeling aspect of relationships. With time and support, some of us can and do learn to conquer our fear, reduce our fixation and minimize our firmness. However, I must warn you that breaking the Fear-Fixation-Firmness Cycle is not an easy process for most men. We operate from a mind over matter perspective, which means we reason first and then feel.

Take Home Message

As you explore your options on the dating scene, remember that some single good men are great candidates, but those who have not conquered their fear are not qualified to be lifetime partners.

**5 Common Types of Fears
Single Men Experience**

Below is a list of the common types of fears that influence men's decisions to avoid lifetime commitment.

1. Fear of Abandonment—occurs when a man is afraid that women will eventually leave them or walk out of their lives. Men in this category will take drastic means to hold onto intimate companionship or avoid it at all cost.

2. Fear of Losing Peer Support and Approval—men suffer this fear because they do not like to be referred to as a sell-out and ultimately lose their peer support. Men in this category dread the idea of changing their lifestyle because they will be viewed differently by their peers. Peer acceptance is important to them.

3. Fear of Changing Lifestyle—men in this category dread compromise and adjustment. They struggle with the idea that they will have to change their lives and be more open to having another person in their life.

4. Fear of Being Emotionally Vulnerable—some men are afraid to share and express emotions out of fear of being hurt. Men in this category typically do not trust women with their emotions or feelings.

5. Fear of Losing Their Freedom—the idea of giving up their independence is anxiety provoking. Men in this category fear that they will be restricted and limited if they commit. They can't sleep with whom they want to sleep with, go where they want to go or buy what they want to buy.

Chapter 2

~

Men Are Skilled in Psychological Warfare, Not Emotional Warfare: Emotions–What Are Those?

"I want to be close to you, but not emotionally. I have been thinking about my future and I want to keep my options open. I like you and want to keep our thing going, but I want you to know that I am not ready for a serious relationship. I am saying this because I care about you and do not want to hurt your feelings. I'm just being honest with you."

How many times have you heard a man say this to you or one of your girls? Many men in the world have spoken the aforementioned words at some point in their lives. By now, you have probably learned that men are skilled and well-prepared to engage in psychological warfare. Some of the things that come out of our mouths make good sense from an intellectual standpoint, but often lack emotional sensitivity. This happens because from the time we are little boys, we receive extensive psychological warfare training, but no emotional warfare training. Let me clarify what I mean.

The average little boy is instructed to "use his head" and to think on an average of forty times a week. When little boys injure themselves, behave inappropriately or make bad decisions, they are quickly reminded of what they should have done differently. They are encouraged to *think*, but are rarely given any guidance about how they should *feel*. And unfortunately, this one-sided instructional process that focuses on nurturing the intellect continues as little boys transition into teens and young men.

Some men hear the words, "Do you ever think?" on an average of sixty times a week. After years of being instructed to think, little boys become men who have crafted the ability to successfully engage in psychological warfare. And before we present something to you, believe me, we have thought about it. We might not always come up with the best solution or sound intelligent, but we often think before we respond. The problem that most women have with men is centered on the fact that we often lack emotional sensitivity, not intellectual aptitude. Learning how to identify and address emotions is challenging for men because we operate in different reasoning spheres from you.

Many of you would agree that men primarily operate from an intellectual sphere and women primarily operate from an emotional sphere. Men are often driven by intellect and believe that facts are as equally important or more important than emotions. Objectivity or impartiality plays a vital role in how men make decisions in relationships. Men typically do not express sensitive or nurturing emotions without apprehension and pre-calculation of the risk. Women are the other hand, are often driven by emotions and believe that feelings are equally important or more important than facts. Subjectivity or emotionality plays a vital role in how many of you make decisions in relationships.

The difference in intellectual and emotional aptitude between women and men is what leads to all-out warfare. Men typically display very high intellectual aptitudes in relationships. In comparison, women typically display very high emotional aptitudes. For example, men speak and behave based on how we think. Our emotional capacity is not necessarily inadequate, but is regularly dominated by our intellect. In contrast, you speak and behave based on how you feel. Your intellectual capacity is not necessarily inadequate, but is commonly dominated by your emotions. Men use intellect to guard our hearts from emotional pain.

We rely heavily on our intellect to cope with, understand and process relationships and life challenges. When we are forced to deal with emotions, we are likely to become frustrated if our intellect fails us. Our desire to rationalize everything typically prevents us from feeling wholeheartedly and subjectively.

Personally, I believe that it is unfortunate that men have become so skilled in the art of psychological warfare. Through socialization, we have learned to rationalize inappropriate behavior, suppress our emotions and engage in tactical warfare in our relationships. We use various intellectual techniques to influence your values, beliefs, emotions and behavior and our ultimate goal is to induce you to do what we want you to do. Through the art of psychological warfare we have learned to manipulate women. This sounds disturbing, right? As I thought about this behavior and surveyed hundreds of men, I found that men engage in psychological warfare, not with the intent to hurt women, but to position themselves in control as they enter relationships.

Too often men will decide to causally hang out with you and demand that you provide all the benefits associated with being in a relationship, but refuse to invest emotionally in you or the relationship. Some men search for ways to take advantage of people and situations in every aspect of our lives, including business ventures and relationships. Scoring what we want in relationships without fighting the fight is the primary purpose of engaging in psychological warfare. We are groomed to be conquerors and to take pride in being able to prevent people, especially women, from scamming and hurting us.

As men, we have definitely learned how to get our "ice-cream" and "cake" by engaging in psychological warfare with you. To illustrate how men are skilled at engaging in psychological warfare, let's revisit and dissect the quote I listed at the beginning of this chapter:

> I want to be close to you, but not emotionally. I have been thinking about my future and I want to keep my options open. I like you and want to keep our thing going, but I want you to know that I am not ready to be serious. I am saying this because I care about you and do not want to hurt your feelings. I'm just being honest.

As you read the quote above, what do you hear and feel? Are you capable of deciphering the message in the quote? This is a classic quote that thousands of men use daily because it communicates interest, foresight, hope, concern, genuineness and honesty. This particular technique is called subliminal persuasion and is designed to influence you emotionally. The ultimate goal is to keep you hanging on.

Men use subliminal persuasion to get what we want while also coming across as being charming. Our messages are very charming and crafted in a positive manner to prevent you from noticing the hidden messages. We want you to think highly of us while doing things that you might not want to do. This is psychological warfare at its best.

Breakdown 1: The Good Message

Sentence #1: He communicates interest—*"I want to be close to you."* Sentence #2: He communicates foresight—*"I have been thinking about my future."* Sentence #3: He communicates interest and hope—*"I like you and want to keep our thing going."* Sentences #4 and #5: He communicates concern, genuineness and honesty—*"I am saying this because I care about you and do not want to hurt your feelings. I'm just being honest."*

Breakdown 2: The Hidden Message

Sentence #1: He communicates that he does not want to be attached—*"but not emotionally."* Sentence #2: He communicates that he wants his freedom—*"I want to keep my options open."* Sentence #3: He communicates lack of interest—*"but I want you to know that I am not ready to be serious.*" Sentences #4 and #5: He communicates honesty to avoid hurting you—"*I do not want to hurt your feelings. I'm just being honest.*"

Some women lack the intellectual aptitude to dissect and understand hidden messages and others just choose to ignore them. This is your biggest mistake when dealing with men, especially good men. It is not easy to dissect the hidden messages of good guys because our tactics are different from those of bad guys. Good guys will express how we feel without sugarcoating our thoughts, but will use positive and inspiring words so that you do not pick up the hidden message. Bad guys on the other hand, will try to manipulate you, but will use negative and belittling words so that you clearly get the message. When a good man tells you that he is not emotionally available or interested in a serious relationship, he will be kind about doing so.

Men are capable of getting our "ice cream" and "cake" because you hear what you want to hear. I would advise you to stop allowing your emotions to control you and start using your God-given intellect. As mentioned previously, men are not as emotionally attuned as you are because most of us have not received proper training. Whether it is right or wrong, we will try to make you feel bad about falling for us because you did not recognize what was being told to you upfront. Remember, most of us operate from an intellectual sphere, and when dealing with men who lack emotional aptitude or are emotionally unavailable, you are likely to experience condemnation for being too emotional.

There is nothing in the world that is more challenging and stressful for a woman than being in a relationship with or having a genuine interest in a man who is emotionally unavailable. Ninety percent of the women I see for individual consultation and marital therapy struggle in their marriages because they are married to men who are emotionally unavailable.

Listen to me when I tell you that men who are emotionally unavailable can and will suck the life out of you and will not experience much distress while doing so. I make it sound as if men are evil and have no heart. This is not the case by far; some men just miss the mark when it comes to recognizing and responding to emotions, especially if they are not truly interested in you or are emotionally unavailable—"Emotions, what are those?"

Some men are emotionally unavailable because they have difficulty recognizing emotions and others choose to be emotionally unavailable because they are consumed by career aspirations, school or work obligations, peer pressure, success, selfishness or heartache from a previous relationship.

Men who are emotionally unavailable do not invest heartfelt time and energy into relationships with women. Your chances of being hurt are greater during this period of emotional seclusion of some men; therefore it is imperative that you learn how to assess whether a man will be emotionally available to you (more on this in Chapter 10).

Emotionally unavailable men want what every man wants—your time, your body, your mind, your companionship and your undivided attention. He wants you to be there for him emotionally, physically and spiritually, but will not give the same in return. Most women do not get or understand this.

Here are a few stories that illustrate how women get hurt by men who are emotionally unavailable.

Story #1

Rob (age 33) and Janet (age 27) have been seeing each other for approximately five months. When they first met, Rob told Janet that he was not interested in having a serious relationship, but wanted companionship. Janet agreed to Rob's terms and they began to hang out on a regular basis. Although Rob had no intention of being with Janet seriously, he still went out of his way to treat her specially. He bought her gifts, took her on trips and wined and dined her.

After several months of hanging out, Janet told Rob that she was starting to fall in love with him and would like to discuss the possibility of having a serious relationship. Rob looked Janet in her eyes and asked, "Why are you getting all emotional and changing up on me now?" Janet was somewhat stunned and replied, "I thought you really liked me because we spend a lot of time together and you treat me really well."

Rob replied, "I was very clear about my intentions from the jumpstart. I treated you like a good man is supposed to treat a woman. It was not my intention to lead you on. What do you want me to do?"

Story #2

Trina (age 27) met John (age 29) while he was in his second year of law school. John was going through a difficult time and was having a hard time staying focused on school. He told Trina that he was interested in having a serious relationship and possibly getting married after law school, but was simply looking for noncommittal companionship for now because he does not want to lose focus.

Trina accepted John's terms. John took Trina to visit his friends and even took her home to meet his parents. John's parents liked Trina, but were concerned that John was being distracted by her. John reassured his parents that Trina was not a distraction because he has no plans to be in a serious relationship any time in the near future.

Four months passed and Trina really started to dig John. She asked, "Do you think there is a possibility of us being more serious with each other? I know you said that you do not want to lose focus while you are in school, but things have changed between us, right?"

John replied, "I like you a lot and things have changed, but I am not interested in being in a serious relationship. I am not ready or willing to dedicate the time that is required to be serious with you. I know I took you home with me to meet my parents, but I agreed to it because you wanted to go. I did not ask you to go."

Who's at fault? Are the men wrong for sticking to their original agreements? If a man tells you that he is emotionally unavailable, pay attention and keep it moving or prepare yourself to deal with the repercussions.

In every relationship, whether it is formal or informal, each individual is responsible for his or her emotions. If the man that you are with has difficulty recognizing and responding to your emotional needs, do not blame him if you stay with him. Learn to establish some boundaries and be firm about what you want and how you want to be treated. Do not expect an emotionally unavailable man to be responsible for or considerate of how you feel. You are responsible for how you feel. Understand that some men are not willing to take responsibility for their actions so it is up to you to protect your heart.

Under no circumstances should you allow a man to attack or demean you for showing or expressing emotions toward him. However, you cannot get mad or upset if he does not show or express the same emotions toward you. God gave women and men the gift of *free will* so that we could think, feel and behave however we want. Therefore, you need to stop trying to persuade men to do things that we do not want to do. You should express your concerns and needs and move on if you are not happy.

Do not play mind games, trying to think like men. You will never be able to think like us, nor should you want to. A man who is ready and wants to be married has already done some preparation prior to meeting you. If he has not taken adequate steps prior to meeting you, he probably will not, and if he does, his actions will probably be for all the wrong reasons—sex or ego stroking.

You know what you want and need emotionally. If a man is not capable of connecting with you emotionally, he should not be allowed to connect with you in any other manner, especially sexually. Healthy marriages are built on emotional intimacy, not physical or intellectual intimacy.

A man's high intellectual aptitude might draw you toward him, but his low emotional aptitude should definitely chase you away. Men who take pride in engaging in psychological warfare in their relationships can become your worst nightmare. Take-heed: when a man tells you that he is not emotionally available—he means just that.

Take Home Message

Some men might be great candidates from an intellectual stance, but without emotional sensitivity, availability and maturity they are not qualified to be lifetime partners.

Chapter 3

Four Marriage Qualities Single "Good" Men Lack

Some men have great qualities and present well in professional, social, familial and interpersonal situations. They shine when interacting with their mothers, sisters, nieces, aunts and female friends. You see this behavior and do not question their ability to enter into and sustain a marriage. You never think to ask yourself, "How can men who are so gentle with and responsive to women be single?" You are mesmerized by their mannerisms and wish that you could be a part of their lives.

Your intellectual blinders are shut tight and you do not want to open them to see clearly. Strong women like yourself like to be challenged, so you convince yourself to believe that you can make any man fall in love with you, especially if you express a little nurturing and sex appeal.

Most of you are convinced that you have what it takes to change a man and believe that you can persuade a man to commit to you and treat you well if you give him enough sex, show him appreciation and submit. This distorted thinking on your part is why most of you have problems selecting and investing in lifetime partners. You fail to realize that your behavior is just a contribution and not the sole or primary factor that determines how men feel, think or behave.

Men are like microwave food. We are prepackaged and appear to be simple, but if you do not read and follow the instructions that are listed on the back of the package, you can screw things up and have a big mess on your hands. As a woman, you can relate to the frustration that occurs when you have your heart and mind set on preparing your favorite dish, but as you begin to cook you realize that you do not have all the proper ingredients. Your lack of preparation prevents you from getting what you desire. Well, as I interact with single men in social and professional settings, I have come to learn that some of them desire to be married, but do not commit because they lack certain ingredients or qualities that are needed to do well in marriage.

Every woman dreams of having a relationship with a man who: 1) is secure in his identity, 2) trusts women, 3) is emotionally resilient and 4) possesses realistic expectations. From the beauty shops to nail shops across America, women express their distaste for men who are insecure, untrusting of women, emotionally rigid and who possess unrealistic expectations. However, many of you end up dating and investing in men who lack the four basic marriage qualities mentioned above. If you want to determine if a man is capable of entering into and sustaining a marriage, you must familiarize yourself with the four basic marriage qualities that most single good men lack. Be mindful that some single good men may lack all four qualities, while others might only lack one or two. The number of qualities that a man lacks is not as important as the behavior that occurs as a result of his deficit.

Identity Security

Failure to develop and to sustain identity security is the first marriage quality that single men lack. In my opinion, identity security in a relationship is not all about a man's ability to accumulate material possessions, provide financial stability for his family and possess certain titles. *Identity security is about conducting oneself like a REAL man by expressing sensitive emotions and demonstrating vulnerability.* A man who is secure in his identity has the ability to cope with doubt, anxiety and fear. He is not preoccupied with losing control by showing his woman that he cares—he does not pretend to be confident, he *is* confident.

The thought of losing control is unbearable for most men. Therefore, we find security in titles and other insignificant things because we feel powerful and in control. We thrive when we are capable of protecting and providing for our family because we feel in control. Many of us feel that we have earned the right and distinct honor of being called a real man if we put food on the table, keep our family members safe, possess respected titles and provide clothing and shelter. According to Steve Harvey, most men are driven by being able to perform and accomplish these things.

I agree, but I would argue that most men are missing the mark on a daily basis when it comes to truly understanding and embracing the role of being a REAL man.

In my guesstimate, thousands of men are misinformed about what it means to be a REAL man; therefore many of us have identity issues and struggle with feeling secure in our relationships. Right about now, you are probably asking yourself, "What makes a man a *REAL* man and what does that have to do with identity security?"

I am glad you asked.

If you pick up any relationship book, search the internet or read blogs about relationships and men, you will probably find numerous definitions about what it means to be a *REAL* man. For example, I have heard women say, "A REAL man gives up one-night stands for a woman he can't stand to live without." I have also heard women say, "A REAL man doesn't play games with a woman's heart." And finally, I have heard women say, "A REAL man takes care of his home."

On a daily basis women and men are having conversations about this topic because there are many definitions and myths about what it means to be a real man. However, most of the conversations that I hear about what a REAL man is and is not are centered on myths about men being macho.

I personally believe that all myths about men should be explored in some form or fashion. However, as a relationship expert, I would be remiss if I did not address the two myths that cause the most damage in relationships: "men are strong and don't show sensitive emotions" and "men are proud and do not apologize." As I debunk each myth, I will highlight how they negatively impact men's behavior and summarize the truths about each myth.

Myth 1: A *REAL* Man Is Strong and Does Not Cry or Show Sensitive Emotions

It is not uncommon for you to hear men say, "A REAL man is strong and does not cry or show sensitive emotions." Men will typically engage in tough behavior to maintain our manhood. Acting feminine by giving freely or expressing sensitive or nurturing emotions is often viewed as being unmanly. The pressure to maintain our masculinity and to remain strong often creates emotional roadblocks for us.

The negative impact: Many men minimize and occasionally suppress sensitive emotions to maintain our masculinity. Often, we become defensive and feel frustrated and angry when someone questions our masculinity. Increased emotional distress experienced by men often leads to a refusal to express sadness or pain in a sensitive or appropriate manner.

Words of affection can be viewed as a sign of weakness and are expressed only in desperate situations, such as at the end of a relationship, a pending divorce or a separation. This insensitive behavior contributes to the conflict experienced in many of our relationships. Instead of saying "I am sorry" or "I was wrong," many of us will allow our relationships to end and even abandon our families.

Many of us have a desire to express sensitive emotions and demonstrate compassion, but lack the ability because we were not trained properly. Our perception of manhood and what it means to be a REAL man is built on false beliefs.

Our primary drive as men is to feel safe and secure. We live, eat and breathe to prove that we are secure in our identities and are capable of dealing with whatever comes our way.

Whether a man is rich or poor, educated or uneducated, his primary goal in life, generally speaking, is to be a conqueror and to be in control. Money, titles and positions are things that we chase after because we feel that we are REAL men once we have acquired them. However, the acquisition of these things does not make a REAL man.

Many men are groomed into believing that the possession of money and titles is what determines manhood. This belief system is what has many of us walking around with self-esteem issues, feeling depressed, unhappy and insecure if we do not have these things. And a large percentage of us believe that we should not marry you unless we are wealthy and can take care of your every need. This is unfortunate because men who acquire material things and titles typically believe we are REAL men because we are capable of providing for and protecting women and children.

The truth: A REAL man is a great provider and protector, but he does not limit his ability to express the God-given emotions he was blessed with. A REAL man will learn to acknowledge and express sensitive emotions in his relationship because he realizes that he gets what he gives. A REAL man eliminates the "tough guy, I don't care" persona because he understands that it will only distance him from you—the woman he loves. A REAL man does not allow this male-dominant society to prevent him from sharing his gift of compassion with you. A REAL man is okay showing affection towards you because he understands that he needs a good balance of emotional expression to have a healthy relationship.

A REAL man does not worry about what other men think about him and will express affection for you when he feels it. A REAL man understands that the expression of sensitive emotions does not convey that he is weak or feminine; it does convey that he is compassionate. A REAL man understands that God created humans, both men and women, with a full range of emotions because He understood that men, like women, could not appreciate happiness without sadness, calmness without anger, laughter without crying, empathy without judgment, and love without hate. A REAL man understands that expressing sensitive emotions is natural and doing so will enable him to share what's in his heart.

Take Home Message

A REAL man is confident, secure in his identity and does not have a problem with opening up to the woman in his life, particularly if it will bring peace into his home and relationship. A REAL man will attend professional counseling or seek some type of guidance if his personal shortcomings are creating distress for him and/or the woman he claims to love.

Myth 2: A REAL Man Is Proud and Does Not Apologize

The one thing I have noticed about men is that we have a hard time saying, "I am sorry." Over the course of more than fourteen years of doing consultation and therapy, I have observed hundreds of women pour their hearts out and explain how and why their men hurt them. They even apologize for doing and saying things that upset or frustrated their men. After they finish speaking, I typically turn to their male counterparts and await a response.

Time after time, I watch men sit with a "what do you want me to say" look on their face and then they respond with solutions and justifications for their behavior, instead of saying, "I am sorry."

For some odd reason there are a lot of men who believe that a REAL man is a proud man who does not apologize. I agree that every man should be prideful; however, no man is too important to apologize to others, especially if they are deserving of an apology.

The negative impact: The Bible says that pride leads to disgrace (Proverbs 11:2), produces quarrels (Proverbs 13:10), leads to punishment (Proverbs 16:5), and destruction (Proverbs 16:18). Men who have too much pride will distance themselves from you and God.

The truth: A REAL man learns humility and is capable of giving compliments and lifting you up instead of tearing you down. A REAL man will apologize to you when he is wrong and will ask for your forgiveness. A REAL man realizes that his stubbornness is a sign of insecurity and will work to address his insecurity.

For many years I have observed and hung out with both married and single men and have noticed some very fundamental differences when it comes to their views about identity security and relationships. Married men who truly understand what it means to be a REAL man show signs of identity security. They are secure in their identities as husbands, heads of households, protectors, providers, lovers and compromisers. They do not feel that they have lost anything by being married. In fact, most of them feel that they have gained something by committing and sharing their lives. They believe in compromising and appreciate the emotional fulfillment that comes with having someone in their lives who compliments them. They do not dread being vulnerable and often boast about showing affection to their women.

Single men, on the other hand, avoid marriage like a plague because they lack identity security. A strong sense of personal identity is important in developing intimate relationships. Men who have a poor sense of self and are afraid of being vulnerable tend to have fewer committed relationships and are more likely to suffer emotional isolation and loneliness.

Guys who are great providers and protectors are great candidates, but because of their inability or unwillingness to be vulnerable and to demonstrate identity security, they are not qualified to be lifetime partners.

Trust in Women

Trust in women is the second marriage quality that single men lack. Trust is an essential part of having a healthy marriage and every woman desires to be with a man who trusts women. However, I believe that trust is difficult for many men because it has to do with how we feel. When we trust women, we open ourselves up and expose our vulnerabilities. This is not easy for many guys, but some of us are willing to be vulnerable if we believe that we will not get hurt in the process of giving up our control.

Trust has many components to it and can be expressed in different ways and toward different people.

Have you ever met a man who appears to be confident and sure of himself when it comes to managing family challenges, career decisions and professional aspirations? As you monitor his mannerisms, he conducts himself in a very reassuring manner and does not demonstrate any sign of being untrusting. However, as you observe and interact with him over a period of time, do you begin to notice that he has trust issues, especially when it comes to being involved in intimate relationships? On the surface he presents well and has confidence that makes him very appealing and desirable. He appears to be marriage material, but the more you interact with him, the more you realize how untrusting of women he is.

I recently had a conversation about trust and women with a single colleague and I was overtaken by his lack of trust in women. As we talked, he mentioned that he would maintain separate bank accounts and would demand that he be able to do what he wants, when he wants. He expressed that most guys get lost in their relationships and marriages and he would not be one of them. He went on to say that he does not trust women and does not intend to lose his identity by entering into marriage and allowing a woman to manipulate him. Every other sentence that came out of his mouth was centered on losing something: his manhood, freedom, money or peer respect. As I listened to the guy, I asked myself, "What the hell happened to him?"

I know a number of single good men who don't trust women and will do whatever they can to keep women at a distance, especially when it comes to men being emotionally vulnerable. Some men might confide in women about issues related to their family and friends, but will not open up personally. This occurs because a number of men lack trust in women because their trust may have been violated during their childhood or in past relationships.

Here are few examples:

John (age 28): My mother left my father for another man when I was 12 years old. My father did not talk badly about my mother, but I did not like her much growing up. Women can be just as selfish as men. I don't trust them.

Eric (age 30): My first girlfriend hurt me when I was 15 years old and at that moment I made a promise that I would never be hurt like that again. I don't trust women. I am not willing to let a woman break my heart again.

Rick (age 36): In my previous relationship I gave more than I received. I never thought someone who is supposed to love me could hurt me that badly. She cheated on me and told me to get over it.

In reading these examples, you can see that men do not open up too easily once our trust has been violated. When we hurt, we hurt! Given this, it is in your best interest to explore whether a man is trusting of women, because a man who has not resolved trust issues from childhood or past relationships will more than likely carry his distrust into future relationships. With this in mind, you need to make sure that you interact with men who have dealt with their trust issues.

Assessing a man's ability to trust is extremely important because men who are trusting behave differently from men who are untrusting. Men who have trust in women are typically free of suspicion and are more prone to cope in a positive manner when faced with adversity in their relationships. A trusting man will show faith in you because he knows that you will do right by him. If you were to leave your phone or email open, a trusting man will not feel a need to look through them. In comparison, men who lack trust in women are more prone to cope negatively when faced with adversity in their relationships. They will not be open and will play mind games with you. Men who lack trust in women are often suspicious and will question your whereabouts. He will probably surf through your belongings and start World War III if he finds some names or information with which he is not familiar.

You can tell if a man trusts you by listening to his tone, observing his behavior and watching his facial expression when he inquires about something that you have said or done.

If you are in a relationship and trust has been damaged, and you are not able to resolve the issue, seek professional help immediately. In all my years of doing therapy, I have never seen a healthy relationship work or last without trust.

Trust sets the stage for love to prosper. Understand that trust must be present and mutually expressed in order to have a healthy marriage. If you meet a man who appears to be charming, gentle and sweet, but lacks trust in women, you should run in the other direction. Regardless of what his reasons are for not trusting women, do not enter into marriage until he resolves them. He might be a great candidate because he is honest about his views about women, but with unresolved trust issues, he is not qualified to be a lifetime partner.

Emotional Resilience

Emotional resilience is the third marriage quality that single men lack. Some men do not enter into marriage because they are not emotionally resilient. Emotional resilience can best be defined as a man's ability to bounce back after experiencing stress. Emotionally-resilient men have the mental ability to return to a previous state of functioning after experiencing emotional trauma. Bouncing back and functioning in a healthy manner after experiencing heartbreak is not likely to occur with most men, especially without some kind of spiritual or mental health intervention. As previously stated, most men are not trained to cope with emotions. So, when we are hurt it is difficult to bounce back. Heartbreak trauma can be very debilitating for men.

When you come across a man who has had his heart broken, you should proceed with caution. There is a good chance that he has not fully recovered. Why do I say this? Many men are not good at dealing with emotions. We are groomed to believe that emotions are not to be dealt with. Simply put, our growing pains are different than yours. For example, if a little boy falls down and scratches his knee, he may be told, "Big boys do not cry." In harsher words, he might be told, "Stop crying, kid; crying is for girls." On the other hand, if a little girl falls down and scratches her knee, she is told, "It is okay to cry" and is often held and kissed. I often get upset when I witness this behavior because *little boys who do not cry become men who do not cry.*

A large percentage of men who get hurt have scars that still need healing. I have talked to thousands of men who have told me that they are still hurting from painful relationship experiences that they had during their teen and young adult years. For most men, heartbreak is difficult to overcome because we lack the emotional aptitude needed to process our emotions in healthy ways. Withdrawing or expressing anger are the two responses that you will typically get from men, especially in times of emotional distress or sadness. The latter emotions are accepted and men are often given passes to demonstrate them instead of being challenged to express an array of emotions.

I believe that a good number of men lack emotional resilience because we passively cope with pain, especially emotional pain associated with bad relationships. Men who cry are sometimes perceived to be weak and women typically do not embrace us if we show too much sensitivity. Therefore, men who are hurt are more likely to be scarred forever. If we have a bad relationship with a woman, we have to pretend that we are not hurting as much as she is. We walk around with open hurt wounds and receive band-aid treatment instead of reconstructive heart surgery. Our scars eventually heal, but not in the proper manner. In talking to guys, I have learned that a man's first heartbreak will haunt him for the rest of his life if he does not have someone to help him understand and process the trauma. Time after time, we are pressured to be "real men" and are frequently reminded to maintain our manhood—"Do not act feminine."

Expressing sensitive or nurturing emotions or giving freely is not praised or encouraged. The pressure to maintain our masculinity and to remain strong often creates emotional roadblocks for us. This means that feelings of remorse, forgiveness, sadness, and empathy are overshadowed by feelings of self-pity, anger, embarrassment, pride, and loss.

While both women and men experience emotional distress, men's coping styles are very passive in nature when it comes to dealing with emotions. Many men are repeatedly instructed to deny or minimize our emotions; therefore we often ignore and avoid dealing with them until they become unbearable.

Men who lack emotional resilience and are not willing to develop active coping skills (more on this in Chapter 13) are not husband material. Do not accept excuses. If a man wants to be with you, he will do what it takes to get you. Request that he attend counseling, seek spiritual guidance, talk to positive friends or do something if he has not resolved or effectively coped with previous or current emotional distress. Remember that emotionally-resilient men see relationship difficulties as temporary and are capable of bouncing back. Some men might be great candidates for dating, but without emotional resilience they are not qualified to be lifetime partners.

Realistic Expectations

The inability to develop and sustain realistic expectations is the fourth marriage quality that single men lack. I recently facilitated a group discussion with fifteen single men and nearly every man who shared his thoughts about women and marriage had unrealistic expectations. When asked, "What do you want in a wife?" the majority of the guys reported that they are looking for a total package: a woman who is extremely attractive, humble, childless, down-to-earth, educated, professional, understands her worth and role, funny, feminine, spiritual and God-fearing, and freaky, but not in public. Most of the group discussion focused on these expectations/qualities and the majority of the guys stated that they want a wife who possesses most of the qualities and are okay with waiting until they find her.

Randy, one of the most vocal guys in the group, blurted out, "I want a wife who looks like Halle Berry, cooks like she is from down South and is educated like the women in D.C. I need all of this. Also, she definitely has to be a professional woman who has money-making potential like me."

After about thirty minutes into the discussion, I shifted the conversation to discuss the roles that they believe women and men should perform in marriage. One guy shouted, "I expect my wife to have my back in everything I do. I want a wife who will give her all, I mean 100%." Another guy shouted, "I agree with him, I want a wife who will provide unwavering support, especially when I am down." As the discussion heated up, the comments came one after the other and all started with "I want" and usually ended with something like "take care of me."

While listening, I heard most of the guys talk a great deal about what they expect to receive from their future wives, but did not hear them talk much about what they would give in return. When I pointed this out and reminded them that devotion to themselves will cause them to remain by themselves, I was told that it is difficult to shift from a "me" mentality to an "us" mentality. I was also told that women have to be willing to ride through the tough times with them and be patient.

I asked, "How do you guys expect to have a healthy marriage if you are not willing to give just as much as you receive?"

One of the guys responded, "For a long time I did not give females an opportunity to get in my space and I still do not now. I don't want too many people to get in my space because I don't want to be hurt. I always have my defenses up and I am always on defense regardless of how sweet a woman might be. I am not going to give a woman an opportunity to hurt my feelings or make me feel bad or ashamed because at the tail end I still have to support myself. So in the back of my mind, I am saying, 'Don't give her everything, give her 75% because she is going to hurt you anyway.'"

As we talked more about their expectations, two common themes emerged: 1) they expect women to be generous, and 2) they expect women to provide 100% unwavering support, but do not expect to be as generous to women and are only willing to give approximately 75% of unwavering support in return.

At the end of the group discussion, I explained that marriage is about giving and receiving and it is irrational to expect to receive 100% of unwavering support and only give 75% in return and expect to have a healthy marriage. I also explained that selfishness and self-centeredness have no place in relationships.

I ended the group session by saying, "Emotional intimacy, trust and mutual respect can only develop in relationships when two hearts are joined and both individuals are giving 100%." The guys concurred with me, but walked away with smirks on their faces.

One of the most difficult challenges some single men face entering into marriage is learning how to be team players who give 100%. This transition is difficult for many single guys mainly because they develop lifestyles, habits and behaviors that are self-serving in nature. Also, a lack of identity security, trust in women and emotional resilience will often lead to the development of unrealistic expectations about marriage. They want you to be close, but not too close.

There are a lot of single guys who avoid marriage or fail once they enter into it because their expectations are not realistic. Some people say that relationships are 50/50. I disagree. Relationships are about being willing to give 100% and understand that some days 50% is all that can be given. Some days we fall short and need help—that is the beauty of having a lifetime partner. The willingness to give 100% is what makes marriage work.

If you meet a guy who expects to receive more than he is willing to give and desires to be with a perfect woman, let him know that he is a great candidate because he knows exactly what he wants, but remind him that he is not qualified to be your lifetime partner.

Part Two

ROADBLOCKS TO MARRIAGE

Chapter 4

Singlehood Is Widely Accepted: Marriage Is Optional

Unfortunately, marriage is not rated as highly as it once was in our society. In this day and age, a lot of women and men feel that marriage is optional. Within the past five years, statistics have shown a drastic increase in singlehood. According to the U.S. Census Bureau's "America's Families and Living Arrangements: 2010," there are 99.6 million unmarried people over the age of 18 in the United States, representing nearly 44% of the adult population. And for every 100 unmarried women there are 88 unmarried men.

The reasons for these alarming statistics about singlehood can be linked to the demographic and economic changes that have occurred as a result of the industrial revolution, the technological revolution and the Women's Movement. Of these three changes that have taken place over the years, the Women's Movement has had a more profound impact on the marriage institution. As women attain more education and seek job security, marriage is being delayed. This shift has impacted the thinking and behavior of single good men because they often do not anticipate that they will meet a "good" woman who is ready for marriage.

Women are making more money than ever before in history; therefore marriage no longer provides the financial security for women that it once did. In fact, many single good women that I have spoken to over the years have informed me that they also dread the idea of marriage because they are afraid of losing assets that they have acquired as successful professional women.

Single "good" men, just like you, are constantly reevaluating the need to get married, especially during their mid-twenties and -thirties because they are focusing on and trying to accomplish professional goals. Making money, living comfortable lifestyles and securing one's future has taken precedence over the desire to get married.

Many men and women say they would like to get married, but their actions are not consistent with their desires. Both men and women are embracing singlehood and are living lifestyles that do not limit their freedom. And unfortunately, the institution of marriage is no longer viewed as an important milestone in the lives of most young adults—marriage is optional.

I recently had a conversation with one of my female friends about the institution of marriage and I asked, "Do you believe that marriage is important?"

She looked at me with a stunned look on her face and said, "Of course, but a lot of women do not see marriage as a viable option. There are not that many good men out here so I am just 'doing me.' If a man comes along and sweeps me off of my feet, then I will get married. I am not in any rush. My career is more important right now anyway. I enjoy hanging out with my girls and dating casually. Marriage is important, but it's just not for me right now, plus I do not have to be married to be happy or have a family."

As I listened to her, I reflected on other conversations that I have had with hundreds of women who felt and thought the same way. After she finished speaking, I told her that she would probably never get married. She looked at me cross-eyed and said, "Excuse me. What do you mean?"

Women, it is simple. Your mindset and attitude about marriage set the stage for how you will live your life and how men will respond to you. If you view marriage as optional, your actions and behaviors will be consistent with your view and men will treat you as an option. Men are good at picking up on women who feel hopeless about marriage. Some men pursue women who talk about marriage, but do not truly believe that it is a viable option. They understand that you will not pressure them to marry you because you are ambivalent about being married and place more value on being single.

They use your ambivalence about marriage and acceptance of singlehood as a weapon against you. They observe your emotional distress as you watch the divorce rate rise. They listen to the distraught conversations you have about marriage with your girlfriends and family members. And, they occasionally provide you with information that highlights that millions of men and women are deciding not to marry, but are living happy lifestyles with benefits.

With a little charm, they convince you to believe that marriage is important, but it's not for you or them. Men advocate for loving you without requirements other than offering you good sex and the reassurance of knowing that marriage might be on the horizon if you stay together.

Single men are reaping the benefits of being part of a sexual revolution that involves high rates of cohabitation, casual dating and unlimited sex. The "get all the sex you can" mindset appears to be the driving force behind the desire to remain single for a large percentage of men and women. Many women and men believe that sex before marriage is a prerequisite to having a good, lasting relationship. Discussions about marriage can be found on most relationships blogs, but people are changing their ways, especially when it comes to managing their sexual desires and energy.

Erica, a devoted blogger, shared this comment:

> I've been pondering the dynamics of marriage and relationships in America for a few weeks as I've been getting to know some people. I'm discouraged that sex is the focus of most things in society and the root cause of so much destruction. If more people could control themselves, just think about how life might be different. Fewer unwanted pregnancies, less crime, and maybe people would get married first before having kids. Anyway, it's a serious matter, but it's kinda making me horny. Lol

The idea of settling down and marrying is becoming more frightening for single good men and women because singlehood is widely accepted. Sexual pleasure is prevailing over traditional values associated with marriage. One of the guys I play basketball with recently told me that he enjoys being single because he is capable of selecting from a diverse pool of women who are okay with having casual sex. Another guy told me that he has difficulty abandoning singlehood because there is no pressure to get married—women accept the fact that he will not commit or be serious with them. Both guys stated that they have a "get sex first, get married afterwards" mentality.

It is without doubt that marriage as a mere option or back-up plan has gained widespread acceptance during the twenty-first-century. Marriage is perceived to be too difficult and single "good" men are choosing to remain single. Everywhere you look, people are divorcing and the tabloids are filled with disparaging stories about bad marriages. This unfortunate phenomenon has caused millions of marriage-minded single men to view marriage negatively as well.

As the single man I once was, I appreciated the benefits of singlehood; however, now, as a husband and marital therapist I do believe that marriage has benefits that are equally as rewarding. I provide eighty percent of the marital counseling in my office and get to see the good aspects of marriage as well. For example, married people have lifetime companionship and reap the benefits of two incomes, two minds and unwavering support for each other when confronted with adversity. But most importantly, marriage makes God happy because He ordained it.

In sum, some single men have difficulty committing to marriage because singlehood is widely accepted and marriage is optional. Society as a whole does not place value on the institution of marriage anymore and single "good" men are going along for the ride. Unfortunately, lifetime commitment is becoming a thing of the past.

Chapter 5

Influenced by Bad Role Models: Married, but Single

"Can married men be addicted to the single lifestyle? Why do some married men act single?" These are questions I receive from married and single women regularly who are baffled about men's behavior.

In talking with married men, I sometimes hear them say that being single was the best time in their life and some still fantasize about singlehood. Rarely do I hear them talk about their marriages, and if they do, I often do not hear the positive aspects. This occurs primarily because many men do not share sensitive stories or emotions with the women in their lives, so sharing with another man is definitely out of the question. Many men are very private, unless we are bragging about our accomplishments, arguing about sports or displaying some kind of hostility toward somebody who upset us. Rarely will you hear a married man talk about how beautiful, kind and intelligent his wife is to another man unless they are in church, at a relationship seminar or attending a marriage retreat.

Single "good" men who have a desire to be married constantly search for answers and information about marriage. It is sad to say, but a large percentage of married men encourage single guys to remain single. This is not true of all married men, but a large percentage of married men do not appreciate their wives in the early stages of their marriages. In many of my encounters with other married men, I often walk away feeling disappointed. The conversations we have about marriage are scary. They make marriage sound like jail sentences and often describe their wives as being wicked and cruel wardens who have total control over them and their relationship.

Consider exhibit A.

Text Message from a Married Colleague

Married guy: Thinking about getting out tonight. What are you up to?

Single guy: Nothing much. Just relaxing!

Married guy: I am going to hit you up later so we can hang out. Maybe go shoot some pool or hit a spot.

Single guy: Cool. Just let me know. Hit me up later tonight.

Married guy: Man, it's around 10 p.m. and I don't think I am going to make it.

Single guy: Why not?

Married guy: My wife wants me to spend time with her; she got an attitude. Man you should stay single so you don't have to deal with this stuff.

This is just one example of how some married men view their wives and marriage. And, in response to what some married men perceive to be hard times in their relationships, many still act single. Some married men cheat and treat their wives like second-class citizens. They come and go as they see fit and brag about being able to do what they want and when they want. Hanging out every other weekend until 3 and 4 a.m. is not viewed by them as being inconsiderate or disrespectful.

When I was single I occasionally hung out with other single guys at local clubs, bars and jazz spots and I was often perplexed by the number of married men who were still hanging out in clubs and picking up women on a regular basis. I was also perplexed by the number of married men who talked about women as if they were not married.

Consider exhibit B.

Text Message from a Married Guy

Single guy: What's up brother? I'm in Arizona until Sunday celebrating my birthday. Let me know if you can meet up.

Married guy: Hey man, where are you in Arizona? I can get out. My wife does not question me.

Single guy: Phoenix.

Married guy: Do you leave on Sunday or Monday?

Single guy: Sunday.

Married guy: I can take you to some hot spots. The ladies are down and have no problem with showing a brother a good time. I get something new every time I go out ... lol. We have a lot of pretty women down here. Really!!! I will hit you later.

Single guy: Cool.

Married guy: Most definitely! My boy James moved here from New York and he is always making it with the women lol. It's rough for a married dude trying to act right LMAO.

Single guy: U can do it.

Married guy: Man I know, but I need God's help lol. That's always been my nemesis: booty LMAO

After reading this, you are probably saying to yourself, "single men can choose to listen to and hang around more positive role models—men who value their wives and marriage."

I agree, and I encourage single men to do exactly what you are thinking—find good counsel. However, I can count on one hand the number of times I have had conversations with men outside of therapy who willingly disclose how they truly feel about their wives and marriage. Given this, single "good" men have a lot to process when it comes to women, relationships and marriage. Some single men want to be married but are not, and some married men want to be single but cannot.

The decision to get married is probably played over and over in the minds of single "good" men at least a million times; however, the images they see are often not good. The divorce rate is over 50% in the United States. Men and women are not honoring their vows anymore and walking away from their marriages like never before. And although some married men set bad examples, single men are not totally discouraged about marriage because of married men's behavior. There are a lot of factors that impact men's decisions in regards to getting married; observing married men who act single is just one of them. In Chapter 8—*The X-Factor: Women's Behavior*, I provide some insight into how women play a role into single men's decision not to marry.

Chapter 6

Single "Good" Men Are Rare Commodities and Have Nice Benefits

Are Single "Good" Men Rare Commodities?

The dating scene is a playground for single "good" men who are in their early- to mid-thirties, successful, educated, childless and financially comfortable. Men who meet these criteria typically reap the benefits of being able to choose from a large selection of women ranging from young to old, unattractive to attractive, uneducated to educated, slim to thick and down-to-earth to high-maintenance. They realize that they are rare commodities and make it known that they have options because there are plenty of women who are searching for them. Men who belong to this perceived "elite" fraternity definitely have great benefits, especially if they are attractive, easy going and successful.

In talking to single men who are "rare commodities," I learned that single men who reside in certain geographical regions or areas perceive that they have better benefits than others. For example, single men residing in the Washington, D.C. and Atlanta areas reported that they have more "quality" to pick from than single men who reside in cities in the Midwest and South. Men from the D.C. and Atlanta areas talked extensively about being able to date women with law degrees, MBAs and PhDs who are also freaky. They boasted about dating women with higher salaries and growth potential. They bragged about having the option to date above and below their economic status.

Many single men say they want to get married, but the single benefits are too great. Being single and a rare commodity means that men can do whatever they want and do not have to consult with anyone; being single means that men do not have to sacrifice or compromise; being single means that men can flirt with and date multiple women; being single means that men do not have to worry about some else's emotional well-being; being single means that men can get as much sex as they want without any strings attached; and being single means that men do not have to cope with relationship stressors.

Of all the benefits that are associated with being a single good man and a rare commodity, the three that were reported to be most rewarding, according to my poll, are as follows: 1) they can have unlimited and unattached sex; 2) avoid the real and/or perceived *stressors* associated with marriage; and 3) enjoy the perks associated with being placed on a pedestal.

Generally speaking, most single good men have difficulty committing to marriage because they love the benefits that single men receive, especially single men who are rare commodities. Some single men truly embrace their singleness and the associated benefits. A 31-year-old bachelor from St. Louis, Missouri reported, "You look at yourself as a high commodity and you should. There is nothing wrong with this and I think women should look at themselves as high commodities as well. I am not going to just settle for anything. There is a difference between compromising and settling. I'm going to seek what I want and women should too."

A 35-year-old bachelor in D.C. shared similar thoughts: "When it comes down to whether or not I think I am a rare commodity for this area or for women in general, the answer is yes, by far. How many African American men do you know that are somewhat successful? I am a single male and don't have any children. Not to say that if I did have children I would not be a rare commodity. I just do not at this time. What it all boils down to is that so many women see this and say, 'Why aren't you married and how can I become a part of your life?' For me the more I become a rare commodity, the more I am able to provide for a woman. Once I get to the point where I do want to be in a full-time relationship and decide to get married, you better believe that it will be with a woman who is also a rare commodity."

Lastly, a 37-year-old bachelor from Atlanta shared his thoughts about being single and a rare commodity: "Being a rare commodity is a special place to be because women have no expectations. So they do not expect you to love them like the everyday Joe because they put you on a higher pedestal. A lot of times men like to stand up there and I am not any different. I like to stand on a pedestal too. However, a lot of women come at me wrong. They'll be like, 'I can buy my own dinner and I can do this and that' because they think that I expect them to be where I am at in life and that is not true. So I am a rare commodity almost by force. Women put me in that box and sometimes I just like being Jack."

I personally think that a lot of single guys who view themselves as rare commodities feel empty on the inside. and To fulfill that void they challenge women and convince themselves that singlehood is not so bad. However, every single man that I interviewed from the East coast, Midwest and West coast appeared to be satisfied with his lifestyle and spoke highly about the benefits of singlehood. For example, Mark, a 28-year-old bachelor from California, had this to say: "The benefit of being single is that you get to go shopping everyday. [laughing] It's like a buffet and you get to be particular. When you get to a certain age, you like quality. When you were probably twenty-one you were okay with buying a rug from Target that was probably seven dollars, but when you are thirty-five you go to Pier 1 because you want that forty dollar rug that is going to last a few years. So that is the thing about being single, you get to pick and choose height, weight, size and shape."

Steve, a 34-year-old actor added, "Are there benefits to being a single good man?—yes there are—but most of the time I don't think we take full advantage of them. I'm not a NBA player, you know what I mean, but I was asked this question just last week. I met this very attractive female and she asked me why I was single. I told her I just am because everybody wants me to be married."

In discussing the benefits of being single with men from various cities throughout America, I have concluded that being a single good man with great qualities is without question a benefit that is highly desired among men in the United States. Committing to marriage is difficult for some men because they believe that a part of being single is being selfish—they can do whatever they want to do and you will allow it.

Chapter 7

~

Men Like to Take the
Path of Least Resistance: Why Get
Married If We Don't Have To?

Some of you often wonder why men hang around, but never marry you. This may come across as being harsh, but Allen, a 38-year-old business owner, asks, "Why get married if we don't have to?" Allen went on to say, "Single men don't have to commit if they are given that option. Some women are looking at their watches and saying it's about that time and some women are not. A lot of men don't have to commit. Like you mentioned earlier, some single men are rare commodities and they know it. So if you don't have to do anything, why would you?"

Reading this must be difficult, but this is a reality because you allow it. I apologize; let me reframe this. Reading this must be difficult, but this is a reality because men decide to travel this path and you choose to be a part of their journey. I reframed my comment because I want you to understand that you are not the primary cause for this kind of behavior. However, you do play a role in influencing men's decision to marry or not, but only as a contributor (more on this in the next chapter).

Most single men do not commit because they like to take the path of least resistance. Taking the path of least resistance means that men will take the easiest way to reach our aims and solve problems, especially in relationships. We engage in this behavior to help save time, and most importantly, to reserve emotional energy.

Unfortunately, a large percentage of men I see in therapy and in my consultation business tell me that they got married because it was the easiest thing to do at the time. This is not to say that they were not in love, but they took the path of least resistance. You must understand what the path of least resistance means to men. This is difficult to figure out because every man operates differently in traveling the path of least resistance. For example, if marrying you will shut you up and take the pressure off, then some men will do just that—path of least resistance. If men can get sex without commitment, then some men will do just that—path of least resistance.

In *Act Like a Lady, Think Like a Man*, Steve Harvey suggested that you must set standards and deploy a ninety-day rule to get the respect you deserve and to determine if a man is worth your time and benefits. He recommends that you ask men the following five questions before you get in too deep: 1) What are your short-term goals?, 2) What are your long-term goals?, 3) What are your views on relationships?, 4) What do you think about me?, and 5) How do you feel about me? He also provided a list of things you could do with your man during your ninety-day plan. I like the questions and suggestions he made and believe that they can help in assessing the commitment issue and determining if a man is truly interested and right for you. However, I think that Steve Harvey forgot to tell you to ask two very important questions: 1) Will you talk to a professional about our relationship? and 2) What are your thoughts about seeking pre-marital or ongoing therapy, if warranted?

These questions will definitely get most men worked up because men are very private beings and do not like talking about their business, especially to strangers. Talking with you and going along with a ninety-day plan is easier than you think for most men; however, talking to others about our feelings, thoughts and background is more difficult.

I am not suggesting that you try to make a man's life more difficult by asking him to do things just to be doing them. However, I have found that when it comes to relationships, men often do not put forth the same effort and commitment as you do.

You can ask your man all kinds of questions and make him wait ninety days in order to assess his worthiness, but I would encourage you to pay more attention to his behavioral tendencies: 1) Does he have a tendency to take the easy way out?, 2) Does he have a tendency to select easy solutions over challenging solutions?, and 3) Does he have a tendency to put forth whatever effort is needed to get the highest reward from his relationships?

Knowing and understanding your man's behavioral tendencies will help you determine if he is worth marrying. Also understanding his tendencies will help you determine if he will jump ship when things get difficult. Women who take the time to learn about their men's behavioral tendencies are successful at walking away before getting caught up. They learn that there is a difference between getting a man and getting a quality man who is willing to work.

In sum, some single men have difficulty committing to marriage because they do not want to invest in women by putting forth the patience, effort or dedication needed to sustain a marriage. Like Allen said, "Why get married, if we do not have to?"

Chapter 8

The X-Factor: Does Women's Behavior Influence Men's Decisions Not to Get Married?

No man can deny the power of a woman. When God created man He knew men could not survive without companionship, so He gave us you, the most precious gift to mankind. God equipped you with gifts that astonish men. You are capable of giving life to the world, comforting the sick, giving moral support, showing compassion, loving unconditionally, standing up against injustice, bearing hardships, carrying burdens, and holding happiness, love and joy.

Simply stated you are special.

Now that I got that out of the way, back to the issue at hand.

Men were created to have dominion over the earth— to rule as conquerors and to lead our wives and children. From a biblical stance, God created man to influence and lead.

However, from the beginning of time, women have had the ability to significantly influence men's behavior, though not always in a good manner. The story of Adam and Eve clearly illustrates the influence and power that women have over men. As you learned in Bible study, Adam disobeyed God because he did not completely embrace and understand his role as the head and allowed Eve to persuade him to do what he was not supposed to do—eat from the Tree of Knowledge.

Now, stick with me as I walk you through the chain of events that unfolded in the Garden of Eden.

On one nice and sunny day, a cool and smooth-talking serpent approached Eve and told her that she should eat from the Tree of Knowledge because it would make her more like God. The serpent also reassured Eve that eating from the tree would not lead to death. Eve hesitated initially, but after thinking about it for a little while, she decided to eat from the tree. After Eve ate, she shared with Adam, who ate as well. Both Adam and Eve knew they had done wrong and decided to hide from God. When approached by God and asked, "What happened?" Adam blamed Eve for giving him the fruit and Eve blamed the serpent for seducing her.

I mention the story of Adam and Eve because it illustrates how women can and do influence men. The story also highlights some of the challenges men and women face in our ability to develop and sustain healthy relationships. Relationships between women and men will never work smoothly as long as individuals allow seduction to prevail over good judgment, lack understanding of their roles, and fail to take responsibility for their actions.

Up until this point, I have explored and informed you about some of the psychological and behavioral issues that influence why single good men decide not to marry. Now it is time to shift gears and talk about the one factor that significantly influences men's decision regarding marriage—your behavior.

In conducting interviews with single men about their difficulty with committing to marriage, every one of them mentioned that women's behavior is among the top five reasons that influence their decisions to remain single. When I asked them to expound, I was told that women are typically placed into six categories based on their behavior. Here are the categories:

Category #1—Deceptive Women

Deceptive women play games with men by either lying or trying to persuade us to believe things that are not true. Some women engage in this kind of behavior with the intent of gaining an advantage over men. The advantage can be either financial or emotional in nature and the deceitful woman always has her own advantage in mind.

"Identifying deceptive women is difficult for men because some women are so deceptive that men cannot tell the difference between women who are truly genuine from those who are deceptive," said Trina, a twenty-four-year-old hairstylist.

The quickest way to contribute to a man's lack of trust in women is to deceive him. Men do not like to deal with women who pretend to be interested in us but are faking. We, as men, love to be promised great things by women and thrive on attention. However, should we find out that a woman had no intention of living up to her promises, we automatically go into an "I don't trust women" defense mode.

Deceit is one of the main reasons so many single good men do not trust women and decide not to marry. Once deceit occurs, trust vanishes and mistrust takes over.

Story #1—Mario

> I will never forget Erica. When I first met her she told me that she really liked me and was interested in getting married. We hung out a lot and she occasionally spent nights at

my place. I remember coming home early one day and heard her telling her girl that she is dating me because she is looking for financial stability. She also told her girl that she was going to use me for money, break me down and leave me because she felt that I was too damn arrogant. For some time, she had me believing that she was truly interested in me. She knew that she did not like me from jump-start, but entered into my circle anyway. Never again will I trust another woman.

Story #2—Andy

Deceit is despicable. My girl Kim told me that she was pregnant, so I proposed to her. I did not propose just because she was pregnant, I truly loved her. I told her that I was not ready for marriage yet, but wanted to do right by her. As we made plans to move forward with our lives together, I started hanging around her more. About five months passed before things went south. I received an anonymous phone call from some guy who claimed that he got Kim pregnant. He told specific details of how and where he hooked up with Kim. I did not want to believe him, but he knew things about Kim's body that someone could only know if they were intimately involved with her. Man, I was disappointed and mad. I approached Kim and asked, "Is that my child inside you?" Kim looked stunned and began to cry. Kim replied, "I let you believe that it was your baby because I did not want to hurt you. I did not mean to be deceptive, but I felt trapped. Plus I did not want to raise a child by myself.

All forms of deceit, whether spiteful or unintentional, are harmful. Knowing something is false and then leading someone down that path is very hurtful. Believe it or not, men hurt more than you think. Some men can forgive women who say things that are not truthful, especially if we do not feel a true connection with you. However, we have a much harder time dealing with deceit when it comes from women whom we are connected to and/or care about.

Category #2—Desperate Women

Men do not like dealing with desperate women and often decide not to marry in order to avoid drama queens. Some of you want to be married so badly that you act too anxious. I have been told that single men get really annoyed when women go out with them on Monday and demand a ring on Friday. Unfortunately, this happens to a lot of single good men. With this in mind, I strongly recommend that you chill out, enjoy dating and let God work for you. Be patient and God will send you a king.

I apologize for saying this, but the older some of you get, the more desperate some of you act. You might disagree and defend your behavior by declaring, "I know what I want and do not want. Plus I do not have time for games."

I did not mention the "age and desperation" correlation to start a debate or to upset you; I simply mention it because some of the single men that I interviewed identify and label older women (35 years of age and older) as desperate because some of you jump on the fast track toward marriage before you get to know them.

Story #1—James

> I went on a dinner date with this attractive lady and I was totally impressed with her demeanor. She was easy going and down-to-earth. After we finished eating dinner, I asked her if I could see her again because I really enjoyed her company. She looked at me and said, "I don't know what you are looking for, but I am not looking to date casually. I did that while I was in college and in my early twenties. I am not looking to get married tomorrow, but I at least want to be in a committed relationship soon. If we hang out again, I need to know where this is going. You look and sound like husband material." After she finished speaking I was shocked. I asked for another date and was informed about her marriage plan. I did not mind the straightforwardness, but her

undertone was not good. I felt like I was in a *Desperate Housewives* scene. I politely thanked her for sharing her thoughts and took her home. As I drove away from her home I 'accidentally' deleted her telephone number.

Story #2—Romeo

My last date was very interesting. She had an overwhelming need to tell me how great she was. She talked consistently about how she could take care of business in the kitchen and did not mind pleasing her man in the bedroom. She talked about being submissive and expressed dissatisfaction about women who do not know how to please men. She told me that she would treat me a like a king if I was her man. And lastly, she told me that she is single because most men can't handle being with a real woman who is confident and knows what she wants. She ended by telling me that she has only been single for a short period and expects to be in another relationship soon. Now mind you, I was somewhat impressed, until I came to my senses and realized that this was our very first date. This woman was desperate. She submitted an application and wanted to be hired on the spot.

Do either of the descriptions above describe you? If you are not sure, let me help you out. You are a desperate woman if you meet the following criteria:

1. You are a lifetime dater and love being in relationships.

2. You establish and maintain strict deadlines about relationships, commitment, marriage and pregnancy and will include any good man into your plan.

3. You often display very anxious behavior around men and dread being single for extended periods of time.

4. You are extremely nice and typically go along with what men want—impressing men is important to you.

5. You consistently seek affection and obsess about commitment and marriage.

Please do not take offense and shoot the messenger if you are a desperate woman.

The sad thing about some desperate women is that some of you will probably make good wives. However, you do not know how to let the chips fall where they must. You cannot treat every good man as if he is the one. As I mentioned earlier, single men get annoyed when you size them up to be your husband without even getting to know them. There is nothing wrong with letting a man know where you stand and laying out your expectations, but hold back on the desperation talk. You do not have to sell yourself. Plus, some men know what we want and don't want, just like you, so please be tactful and monitor what comes out of your mouth.

As you can see based on the few responses listed above, many men will not hang out with or get to know a desperate woman. Therefore, I encourage you to enjoy the date and keep a level head—no marriage talk on the first date. Only three things happen to desperate women—they get hurt, taken advantage of, or left alone to prey on other men. As your personal relationship coach, I strongly advise you to reevaluate your approach if you fall into this category—this is hard to say, but you scare men.

Category #3—Damaged Women

Some men avoid marriage because they do not want to deal with women who have been damaged from previous relationships. Women still hurting from their previous relationship have a tendency to bring baggage with them into their new relationship. A bitter and hurt woman is not easy to deal with and most men prefer not to get involved.

Story #1—Eddie

Most women think that there are no good men out here because they have been hurt in past relationships. My girl brought a lot of baggage with her. I am not saying that I am perfect and don't make mistakes, but I do not hold her accountable for the actions of other women. She is different! I am constantly reminded of how the other guy did this and that to her. I try to be sensitive, but I have a hard enough time trying to make up for my own mistakes, so I sure can't make up for another man's mistakes. After about three months of hearing about past drama, I jumped ship. I can be miserable by myself. They say misery likes company; well I don't need or want that kind of company.

Story #2—Ronald

I met Stacey, a single mother of two children, through a mutual friend. When I first met Stacey, I thought she was a good catch because she was a good woman. She took care of her business, her children and was a trustworthy woman. I liked her nurturing and down-to-earth spirit. She was very good with her children. I did not see any concerning flaws until we started dating seriously.

I remember when the drama started. I asked Stacey to marry me after dating for one year. On the day I proposed, her emotional issues began to surface. She went off on a tangent about how she has been hurt before by the father of her children and is not going to go through that again. I was shocked because I had done everything in my power to reassure Stacey that I would not abandon or hurt her. Plus we had this conversation at least forty times within the past year. I suggested that we seek counseling on several occasions, but Stacey did not feel that she needed any help and told me, "I am a little scared, but you need to understand that I will probably struggle with this fear for the rest of my life." Although I cared about Stacey, I was not willing to subject myself to a lifetime of misery. She was holding me in hostage mode because of what some other man did to her. I called off the engagement and moved on. Love lost, but peace of mind gained.

I realize that it is difficult to recover from pain or hurt, but I assure you that no man wants to deal with unresolved relationship grief or pain. Now you might say, "A real man will stand by his woman and help her work through her problems." I agree, partially. I can tell you from personal and professional experience that having a damaged soul is like living without an identity. I have observed men try to modify their actions to provide comfort and security, but have had little success. A man can love a woman, but a woman will not get over her pain until she is ready and willing to be loved. Unresolved bitterness and pain can keep men at a distance. Who wants to marry a damaged woman?

Category #4—Independent Women

As a single man, I often met women who made sure that I knew that they could open their own car door, pay their own bills, fix things around the house and satisfy their own basic sexual needs if warranted. As a married man, I am glad that I do not have to deal with the new twenty-first-century women anymore—women who are too independent.

During the twentieth century, women allowed men to do things for them because they desired, demanded and respected chivalry. Nowadays, women are quick to remind men that they "do not need them." I agree that you do not need a man, but if you want a man, especially a husband, please stop acting so independent. What do I mean?

I am not suggesting that you bow down to a man and act as if you cannot do anything for yourself. I am simply suggesting that you allow a man to be man. Respect what he brings to the table. I know you have heard this a million times, but hearing something and understanding it are different. Understand that some men take great pride in treating women like a queen. And I am not talking about buying you material things.

There is nothing more attractive to a man than being with a woman who knows her role and worth. A woman

129

who knows her role and worth will allow her man to support her and will support him in return. Coretta Scott King exemplified this behavior and set the standard for women like Michelle Obama to follow.

Stop screaming, "I can do it" and start screaming, "I can do it, but it would be nice if you helped or did it for me." The "I Am an Independent Woman" persona is not attractive at all.

Story #1—Ronald

> I met Angie at a social event for young professional adults. We started hanging out on a regular basis shortly after meeting at the social. Every time we hung out she bragged about how she makes just as much money as men do and holds a high position in her organization. Initially, her boastfulness bothered me, but I ignored it because I figured that she talked that way to either impress me or to remind me that she does not need me. I did not mind mingling with Angie because I like confident women who are capable of taking care of themselves. I think it is sexy. However, as time passed Angie insisted that we split the bills whenever we would go out to eat. I informed Angie that I did not mind paying for her dinner occasionally because I enjoyed her company. Angie told me that she has been doing things for herself for so

long that she does not know how to accept chivalry.

Story #2—Ronald

I recently met this young lady for our first date and she went on and on about how she could do this for herself and do that for herself so I asked her why would she need a man. She looked at me and replied," You want me to be honest. Other than fulfilling my sexual needs, I would have to think about it. My father taught me to be very independent, so I don't require a man to do much for me." That was our first and last date.

Most women get defensive when men start talking about the "independent woman" issue. I personally believe that women who struggle with this issue do not understand their roles. A woman can be self-sufficient without making a man feel unwanted. Furthermore, a real man does not want you to feel inadequate or inferior so that he can feel empowered. Stroking a man's ego is not a bad thing, especially if he is stroking yours in return.

Learn to humble yourself and accept chivalry. I can tell you that there is nothing more annoying to a man than going out with a woman who brags about being able to take care of herself, but she never reaches for the bill after eating dinner. This happened to me a few times and I wanted to say, "If you are that independent, then pick up the tab." Now some women don't have a problem with this, but that is not my point. I know you all are capable of doing things for yourselves. That is easy. The challenge for most independent women is developing the willingness and ability to allow men to cater to you.

With all the game-playing that is happening these days, I realize that it's hard to let your guard down and to accept kind gestures from men, but this "independent woman" thing is too much. The "independent woman" concept is anti-relational in my opinion. The last time I checked, human existence has been sustained throughout history because men and women continue to rely on each other. Sharing and depending on each other is what makes relationships blossom, not individuality. A Proverbs 31 woman is skilled and makes her own money, but she brings it home for enhancement and supports her partner. She does not brag about her skills or resources and she definitely does not compete with her partner.

The song "Independent Women" was a national anthem for women in 2000 and ignited a spark among millions. Women all around the world developed the courage to step out on their own with confidence, but as they say, all good things must come to an end—I guess Beyoncé even got tired of being an independent woman (go Jay-Z).

Category #5—Jump-Off Women

This category of women has supernatural power over single good men. At a comedy show in St. Louis I heard a comedian define a *jump-off woman* as a woman whom a man can tell anything to and she will let him jump off into her. He also mentioned that jump-offs are usually first cousins of Gold-Diggers. I tried not to laugh, but every man in the audience was laughing heavily, especially the single guys.

The comedian went on to say that jump-off women are like nymphomaniacs: they love to have a lot of sex and as often as possible. According to the comedian, jump-off women are mostly impressed with a man's title and want nothing more than to be in the physical presence of a successful, ambitious and attractive man.

As I heard the comedian talk about this category of women, I was somewhat bothered because there are millions of women who fall into this category, and they make it easy for single good men to avoid marriage.

Story #1—Pete

I met Sandra at my boy's birthday party on Friday and I called her Sunday. She stopped by the house late Sunday evening and we were having sex within two hours of her arrival. She told me that she was impressed with the way I carried myself. She told me that she is only attracted to men who have their heads on right. I could not believe that she was that easy. Usually the successful women try to run game and hold out, but not her. Man the world has changed drastically. Some women do not have a problem with giving it up.

Story #2—Anthony

What single man in his right mind would turn down easy sex? Just last Saturday I met this young lady at Home Depot and she told me that she likes guys who are handy. We sparked up a conversation and I asked her out. She agreed and we decided to meet on Tuesday evening for dinner.

Tuesday came around and we met at a nice restaurant. Nothing too fancy or expensive, but very nice. We had great discussions about various topics (relationships, politics, etc.) and I was truly impressed with her. At the end of our date, she asked if I wanted to go back to her place for light refreshments. Of course, I agreed. Shortly after we enjoyed some chocolate covered strawberries, we pleasured ourselves by having some hot and careless sex. Man, jump-offs are God's gifts to single men.

If you fall into this category, please seek some professional counsel. I do not mean to judge you, but your behavior will never provide you with the kind of happiness that you deserve. Having casual sex might fulfill a sexual need for you and your temporary partner, but you will never be respected or viewed as a keeper. Single men might love spending time with you, but don't even think about lifetime commitment.

Category #6—High-Maintenance Women

High-maintenance women are usually attractive women who serve as good trophies for single men, but are too expensive to marry. They typically have perfectionist tendencies and spend an excessive amount of time, money and energy trying to maintain a perfect appearance. Their nails, makeup and hair must be on point all the time (daily) and they will do whatever is needed to maintain their youth, femininity and beauty. They are more likely to have surgical procedures performed (breast implants, skin treatments, etc.) and normally view men as moneymaking machines.

High-maintenance women are very selective in whom they date and are often perceived to be bougie. They expect their men to drive certain cars, live in certain areas and have unlimited assets. This category of women can consist of highly educated, professional women or uneducated ghetto women. Their primary goal is to find a man who can assist them in developing or sustaining a fabulous lifestyle. Most of the women that fall into this category feel that they are entitled to be happy, a happiness they achieve by pressuring men into buying them expensive gifts, cars, clothing, and jewelry. Although some of these women can take care of themselves, they will not entertain men who cannot take care of them or keep them happy.

Most single men who like "average women" typically date high-maintenance women for showcase purposes and rarely take them seriously or marry them. Even guys who are financially stable and can afford high-maintenance women often report that they do not commit to them on a long-term basis because they do not like to deal with their personality quirks.

Story #1—Tim

> I briefly dated this female who was high maintenance. She was very attractive, but acted bougie as could be. My sisters and

aunts did not like her because she acted as if she was too good to interact with them.

Her father owned a couple of clothing stores so she was used to getting what she wanted. Whenever we would go out to eat she ordered the most expensive food, wine and dessert, but she never offered to pay for anything. On average, I would spend two- to three-hundred dollars each time we went out to dine (sometimes twice a week). I remember asking her why she always chooses fancy restaurants and she told me that she does not eat at cheap restaurants. After hanging out with her for a few months, I realized that I could not afford her company. I mentioned that I might need to break things off and she told me that she did not think that I could afford her anyway. I was not mad at all. My savings account increased with the loss.

Story #2—Peter

I did not know Jennifer would be so high maintenance when we first met. She was a nice looking young lady, but did not come from "old money." She grew up in a middle-class household in the suburbs. So I was amazed by her unwavering desire to shop at expensive stores. Nordstrom was one of her favorite stores. I remember going shopping with her and she asked me to buy her a handbag. I did not mind, so I told her yes.

> She walked down the aisle and came back with a Lanvin handbag that cost $3,685.00.
>
> I am not going to tell you what I said to her, but I will tell you that we did not talk again after that day.

As a woman, you have the ability to influence men in many ways. Everything that you do significantly impacts us in one way or another—everything you do matters to us. Men might not tell you initially, but believe me, your actions have power.

Men place women in categories because it helps us make sense out of your behavior; as you can see, there are certain categories in which you do not want to be placed. Single men make up a lot of excuses as to why they refuse to get married and why they struggle with commitment, but the most influential factor is your behavior—you are the X-Factor.

Part Three

The Investment:
How to Get What You Deserve –
Lifetime Commitment

Chapter 9

~

Determine If You Can Offer
Quality Time: Men Require and
Need Attention

Make sure that you let your partner know that spending time with him is your top priority. Why is this important? Men are more likely to marry women who make time for them, strive to understand them and express that they have their best interest at hand. As a therapist, I talk and listen to married men daily and find out more about them all in one hour than their wives do in five or ten years of marriage. I am capable of establishing this bond as a therapist because I offer quality time, not quantity. As a single good woman you probably cook, clean and make good love to your partner, but unfortunately you will never get lifetime commitment if you do not offer quality time. Meeting your partner's physical needs is only part of what God expects of you. You must also offer quality time, which involves being attentive to your partner's emotional, spiritual and psychological health so that he can lead you in a healthy manner. Proverbs 31:12 states, "For she employs all her living for her husband's good." Undeniably, men are not complete in and of ourselves. This is why God created you.

So how do you determine if you are offering quality time?

You should be able and willing to sit down and listen to what is on your partner's mind. A woman who offers quality time has a genuine interest in trying to understand what motivates and drives her partner. However, you can only do these things if you take the time to ask: "How are you feeling? How was your day? How are you doing? How can I help you? Is there something I can do to make your life and our relationship better?

You should be having conversations with meaning. If you are not having interactions with meaning, then you are not necessarily offering quality time. *Quality time involves a certain level of attentiveness.* You should know what your partner needs and wants from you and you should be willing to explore and entertain his needs. I am not suggesting that you devote all of your time and attention to your partner, but I am suggesting that you should be able to hear him out when he is in need. Believe it or not, a woman who devotes her time to a marriage-minded man is more likely to get a formal commitment.

Offering quality time is one of the most precious gifts that a woman can offer her lifetime partner, especially after the motherly demands and duties begin. Over the course of my career as a marital therapist, I have heard thousands of married men complain and become extremely frustrated because their wives do not spend time with them or listen to them. As I processed what they were saying to me, I learned that most married men want to be heard and want attention. It is without question that we all feel better when we are heard and attended to. Therefore, I believe quality time has to do with a woman's willingness and ability to devote time to listen to her partner and to address his need for affection and attention.

Have you ever asked yourself why do some single men go out of their way to be noticed by women and do whatever is needed to get attention? According to Abraham Maslow, a renowned psychologist, all humans have five basic needs: physiological, security, social, esteem and self-actualizing. Men are typically capable of addressing our physiological needs: water and food. Also, men are typically capable of addressing our safety and security needs: protection from harm and shelter from the environment.

However, of all the basic needs presented by Maslow, social needs (which include the need for belonging, love and affection) best explain why so many of us go out of our way to be noticed and admired by you.

The need to belong and to feel valued is an intense social need that dictates how most men behave the majority of the time. Some men will do whatever is required to feel valued and to get attention. Men's deeply felt need to be appreciated, respected and valued can best be understood by paying attention to our passive/aggressive, cold and sometimes destructive behavior when we feel neglected.

Once you understand and accept that your partner craves and needs attention, your ability to understand and influence him will be met with less resistance. If you fail to make time to nurture your partner's emotional, sexual and spiritual needs, some other woman will. In today's fast-paced, self-sufficient and unstable society, marriage-minded single women, like you, are devoting an excessive amount of time on building your careers, enhancing your social status and securing your financial future. Because a large percentage of single women are consumed with achieving the above-mentioned goals, you occasionally neglect your partner's social need for quality time—attention and affection.

Regrettably, this universal problem affects thousands of single women on a daily basis, especially those who have a strong desire to be successful, stable and grounded in life. Obsessed with career success and financial security, some single women believe that working is as equally important as spending time with their partner.

Balancing relationship and career aspirations can be a challenge for single women. Work and life demands can consume a large percentage of your time. However, if you desire to have a lifetime partner, you must offer quality interactions. Relationships grow when individuals address and meet each other's need for attention. You can accomplish this task by having meaningful and quality interactions with your partner. Quality interactions enable both men and women to influence each other's thinking and behavior. This is because greater understanding occurs when individuals can relate to and empathize with each other. Being a stable and self-sufficient woman is great, but if you do not have to spend time with your partner, he will probably think twice about marrying you.

Steve Harvey encourages you to set some standards so men will fall in line and give you what you want—the ring. While it is important to get the ring, it is equally important to offer quality time. In my line of work, I interact with thousands of women who have received their rings; however, a large percentage of their husbands are not happy because they do not offer quality time.

You can give your body, labor and money, but remember that emotional intimacy develops as a result of quality interactions. As a matter of fact, sexual intimacy, physical labor and financial status have little impact on how individuals behave in marriage, especially if nothing is done to stimulate or nurture the love in their hearts. If you desire lifetime commitment, strive to bond with your partner by connecting with your heart.

How many times have you heard the saying, "Money cannot buy you love?" This is true. Unfortunately, wealthy and self-sufficient single women experience just as much hardship on their quest to invest in a lifetime partner as poor single women. This is because marriage occurs through meaningful interactions—quality time, not by giving of your body, labor or money. If you want to get what you deserve, offer your partner quality time.

Chapter 10

Learn the Basics about Men's Emotional Temperament

You don't need to know everything about men's emotional temperament, but you do need to learn some basic terminology so that you can be better equipped to invest in a lifetime partner. Men's emotional temperament has to do with our natural emotional makeup or predisposition. Some basic terminology to describe this includes "emotionally available" and "emotionally unavailable." Do not remain in a relationship with an emotionally unavailable man, thinking that you are going to change him. If your partner tells you that he is not looking to get married, bells should ring and you should move quickly to remove yourself from the relationship. Some men will tell you where they are emotionally and some will not. With this in mind, it is imperative that you learn how to identify, assess and walk away from men who are emotionally unavailable. Believe me, it will save you a lot of heartache.

Identifying Emotionally Unavailable Men

There are three categories of emotionally unavailable men: 1) those who are emotionally unavailable by choice, 2) those who are emotionally unavailable because they are afraid of being hurt or feel vulnerable, and 3) those who are emotionally unavailable by choice due to fear.

By Choice: Men who choose not to be available emotionally are frequently consumed by desires to pursue and achieve career goals. Their decision to remain emotionally unavailable is significantly influenced by their decision to focus on their careers or other areas of their lives. They understand and are okay with putting their personal lives on the back burner, and make it known that they are not available.

Fear: Men who are afraid of being emotionally available do not make a conscious choice; they are driven out of fear of being vulnerable or being hurt. They desire to be in relationships, but their fear consumes them. They desperately want and believe in companionship, but are afraid to go get it. Men who are afraid cope with their fear by putting their professional life in the forefront.

By Choice Due to Fear: Some men make themselves emotionally unavailable by choice due to fear. Men in this category desire to be in relationships, but choose to remain single out of fear. They are typically financially comfortable or stable and their careers are on track. They will talk about commitment, but will not take serious steps toward committing.

I identified three categories because I want you to understand that the reasons men give for being emotionally unavailable really do not matter–they all have devastating effects. Some of us believe that choosing to be emotionally unavailable due to career aspirations is more acceptable and manly than operating out of fear. Often we will tell you that we are focused on our careers or other issues, but a large percentage of men, in my opinion, are emotionally unavailable due to fear.

Assessing Men's Emotional Availability

If you listen to men talk about their past relationships, most will share stories about women who have either directly or indirectly hurt them or broken their hearts. It could have been a female relative (mother, sister, etc.), a close female friend or their first love. In talking with men in various professional and social settings, I found that emotionally unavailable men typically have experienced some emotional pain and decide to remain emotionally detached to prevent the pain from recurring.

I recently had a conversation with a young lady and she asked me, "How can I determine if a man is emotionally unavailable and what should I do? What does it mean when some guys choose not to be emotionally available?" Here are the answers:

Emotional unavailability describes a man's mindset. Identifying emotionally unavailable men is fairly easy. There are five major behavioral indicators that I encourage women to consider: 1) Does he keep his guard up or have trouble sharing his emotions, 2) Has he been in a long-term committed relationship within the past two to five years, 3) Is he approaching or past the age of 35 and still single, 4) Does he spend a significant amount of time focusing on school, work or other areas of his life and is only open to companionship that meets his terms, and 5) Does he engage in self-serving behavior and express little concern for other's emotional needs?

If a man answers yes to one or more of the behavioral indicators listed above, then there is a high possibility that he is an emotionally unavailable guy.

Emotionally unavailable men look, act and think like any other man, but experience difficulty in entering or sustaining relationships because they are extremely sensitive to being hurt. If he becomes defensive when discussing emotions, he is probably experiencing some mild fear or anxiety.

Some emotionally unavailable men deal with fear by becoming high achievers. Also, they might get involved in heartfelt community and church activities to feel emotionally connected to others in some way.

What is interesting is that most emotionally unavailable men are very compassionate and thoughtful. This is where it gets tricky for you. What woman does not want a compassionate and thoughtful man? You long to be in a relationship with a compassionate and thoughtful guy and will spend your whole life looking for him.

Emotionally unavailable men are not bad individuals, they simply lack the skills needed to direct their compassion and thoughtfulness toward women, especially in intimate relationships. Limiting their love and holding back are defense mechanisms.

If your man is not emotionally available, do not invest your time, especially if he is not willing to acknowledge or meet your emotional needs (more on this in Chapter 13).

Keep in mind that no relationship can blossom without emotional bonding. Assess for emotional availability by using the behavioral indicators mentioned above and move on if the man you are interested in is not available. Whatever you do, do not say "I do."

> **Emotional Availability**
> **Knowledge Quiz**

Let's see if you can identify the different categories of men's emotional availability. Circle the correct answer for each question. The answers are listed at the end of the quiz. Good luck.

1. "I am focusing on my career right now, but I make time for important people in my life. I like dating and believe that women are nice to hang out with, but I usually do not disclose my inner thoughts or feelings."

   Emotionally Available or Emotionally Unavailable

2. "I recently got out of a bad relationship, but I am not bitter. Things happen for a reason and I have taken time to heal. I am optimistic and feel that I am still capable of loving again."

   Emotionally Available or Emotionally Unavailable

3. "Having standards is okay, but women want too much. They must also remember that no man is perfect. Too much time is spent talking about how they feel. I want to

be there for my woman, but I get tired of being sensitive."

Emotionally Available or Emotionally Unavailable

4. "I can't be with a woman who is extremely emotional. Subjectivity is important, but women need to get a grip."

Emotionally Available or Emotionally Unavailable

5. "I have been hurt before and now I have a list of conditions women must meet before I let my guard down. I am afraid of getting hurt so my future wife will have to work hard to win me over."

Emotionally Available or Emotionally Unavailable

6. "Often we fail to realize that relationships should be built on love and respect, not perfectionist tendencies. It does not make sense to withdraw or limit love because you are not happy. Life and relationships are filled with ups and downs, but mutual respect and understanding can help."

Emotionally Available or Emotionally Unavailable

7. "Men should strive to love their women despite their shortcomings. I want to be with a woman who will also hear me out and accept my shortcomings. I feel whole when I have a woman who encourages and wants me to express my emotions."

Emotionally Available or Emotionally Unavailable

8. "If I tell a woman that I am focused on other areas in my life, she should not get upset. If I make it and become successful, she will benefit as well."

   Emotionally Available or Emotionally Unavailable

9. "I enjoy spending time with my woman. I do not always understand her feelings, but I try to demonstrate empathy. I listen and share my emotions and thoughts about the situation."

   Emotionally Available or Emotionally Unavailable

10. "I grew up in a household where no one expressed how they felt. Doing things for each other was more important than sitting around talking about feelings. My wife wants me to listen to her when she is sad. I would prefer to take her out. I don't do well with the feely stuff. "

    Emotionally Available or Emotionally Unavailable

For answers, see next page

1. Emotionally Unavailable

2. Emotionally Available

3. Emotionally Unavailable

4. Emotionally Unavailable

5. Emotionally Unavailable

6. Emotionally Available

7. Emotionally Available

8. Emotionally Unavailable

9. Emotionally Available

10. Emotionally Unavailable

Chapter 11

Study the Risks: His Lifeline and Ambition

Take note of your partner's lifeline and ambition. These are risk factors that you should study and understand prior to investing. If your man tells you that he wants to marry you but most of his friends are single and he continues to hang out with them to the clubs or wherever they go, then you really want to pay attention to his crowd. This is important because single men typically do not transition into married life by hanging out with single men. Some people might not agree with me, but I truly believe that men who are looking to get married have to change their environment and reduce the frequency and time they spend hanging out with single men, especially if they are not marriage-minded single men.

His Lifeline

Your partner's social circle can tell you a lot about him. You probably agree that most of us hang out with people who are usually representative of who we are. If your partner does not disclose much information about himself, pay close attention to the behavior of the men he considers his good buddies.

Women often tell me that they do not find out about their men until they have dated them for an extended period of time or until they have jumped the broom. This occurs because most women do not know what to pay attention to.

If you pay attention to and take note of how your partner interacts with and responds to the influential people in his life, you can get a very good understanding of how he is likely to act in a relationship. Consider Amy's story below:

> When I first met Randy I knew we would not have any problems entering into and sustaining a relationship because he was a good guy who respected women. However, after several dates I started to see Randy's true colors emerge. Randy never did or said anything that personally concerned me when we were alone, but I noticed that he responded to and treated me differently when he was around Lance, his best friend from childhood. Lance was nice to me, but he did not think highly of women in general.

Lance had a tendency to talk down to women and respond to them in a very hostile, negative and disrespectful manner.

I did not want to judge Randy based on Lance's behavior, but I should have paid closer attention. On the surface, Randy appeared to be totally different from Lance, but the more we hung out, I saw strong similarities. One of my girlfriends told me that Randy was not right for me because Lance had too much influence over him. Randy respected and looked up to Lance because he was a successful business man and did not take nonsense from women. Randy did not think that Lance was a bad guy and often became defensive whenever anyone said something negative about him.

I should have stepped back when I heard Lance curse women and Randy never said anything to disagree with him. At times I felt disrespected by the way Lance treated women and I told Randy, but nothing was said.

I remember getting into a disagreement with Randy and he cursed at me like I was a stranger off the street. I was totally surprised because in three months of hanging out, I never heard him curse. I asked him why he talked to me that way and he told me that he is not going to take any nonsense from me. Initially, I did not want to believe that Randy was like Lance, but I found out the hard way. I guess the saying "birds of a feather flock together" is really true.

The purpose of sharing Amy's story is to remind you of the importance of paying attention to the company that your partner keeps. Understand that we are all by-products of our social circles and environments. If you fail to take into account your partner's social circle and family dynamics, you will fail to capture a very important aspect of who he is.

Pay attention to your partner's lifeline: individuals who motivate and inspire him (mother, father, friends, etc.). You should explore this issue extensively before you say. "I do." Most men value and find security in relationships that we have developed and maintained for many years. Individuals who are close to us play major roles in how we behave and think. With this in mind, you must pay close attention to your partner's circle. If he is honest with himself and truly desires to make a change for the best, he will limit the amount of time he hangs around guys who might influence him in a negative way.

As I began to prepare myself for marriage, I reduced the amount of time I spent with other single guys. I made this decision because their minds were focused on hunting and conquering women. I realized that I had to change my lifeline if I wanted to make a smooth transition into marriage. This decision was not easy because I was teased by the fellows. I dealt with the teasing and stuck to my decision because I realized that I could not do the same things and expect that I would change suddenly after I was married.

Knowing your man's lifeline is critical. Many women do not pay attention to men's lifelines or have no idea of how to extract this information from them. The five following questions will help you:

1. If we were to get married, who would be your best man?

This person is important to him and has probably been a part of his life for some time. This is someone he cares about and will probably turn to in the future. Get to know this person.

2. Who is the most important person in your life?

It's important to sort out who he feels plays a major role in his life. This person will definitely provide input regarding issues in your man's life.

3. Do you have a mentor?

Check to see if he has a mentor: a professional mentor or personal mentor. This individual will also give him advice. Most women underestimate the role that mentors play in men's life. We are more prone to listen to men who we believe are wise.

4. Who do you go to when you need advice about relationships?

Make sure that you know who he considers to be a relationship guru. This person will typically provide him with information about relationship issues.

5. How would you manage a conflict between your future wife and the most important person in your life?

This question is critical because it will help you understand where you stand in comparison to the most important person in his life. This question will also give you an idea of the kind of influence the person has over your partner.

Asking these questions is critical to assessing your partner's lifeline. If you decide to get married and do not pay attention to your partner's lifeline, you will pay for it later. If you are bothered by your partner's lifeline and he does not feel a need to address or respond to your concerns, do not invest more time—exit immediately.

His Ambition

Is your partner strongly influenced by success, money, financial stability, titles, material items or fame? In our society most men are influenced by these things and women love to date men who are driven and ambitious. However, many of you fail to understand that men who are influenced by the things listed above are more likely to struggle in their marriage, especially if they do not know how to balance their lifestyles.

There is nothing wrong with dating a man who is influenced by success, money, financial stability, titles, material items or fame, but know that you will likely have problems if he is not also strongly influenced by the desire to have a healthy marriage or family. Through intimate conversations, you can get a good idea of whether your partner's values are consistent with yours. I often suggest that women develop a list of values and rank them.

The list could include the following values: a) financial stability, b) success, c) hard work, d) honesty, e) helping people, f) healthy relationships, g) health, h) material items, i) mutual respect, j) education, and k) emotional support. After developing your value list you should compare them to your partner's list. See example below.

Your Values	Your Partner's Values
1. Helping	1. Financial Stability
2. Relationships	2. Success
3. Hard work	3. Hard work
4. Honesty	4. Health
5. Health	5. Honesty
6. Success	6. Helping
7. Financial Stability	7. Relationships
8. Material items	8. Material items

Rank your values from the most to least important:

Your Values   Your Partner's Values

1. _____   1. _____

2. _____   2. _____

3. _____   3. _____

4. _____   4. _____

If your values differ significantly from those of your partner, as reflected in the example above, you should seriously consider moving on.

You must remember that the things or values that influence a man before he marries you will also influence him after he marries you. So make sure that your values align with your partner's values. If you find that you do not like the risks associated with who and what influences your partner, do not invest—remain firm in your beliefs and exit immediately.

Chapter 12

Explore His Motivation for
Marriage: Internal or External

Explore whether your partner is internally or externally motivated before you invest. In working with hundreds of men over the years, I have learned that men's decision to enter into marriage stems from two sources of motivation: internal and external. Understanding whether your partner is internally or externally motivated is the first step in determining if he is ready for marriage. Once you identify your partner's source of motivation, you will be better equipped to determine if he is worth the investment. Furthermore, you will learn how to respond to him appropriately.

External Motivation

Unfortunately, large percentages of men decide to get married because of external motivation. External motivation is based on societal and interpersonal influences. A man who is externally motivated is more likely to marry you because society tells him that he has reached the point when he should settle down and get married. External motivation may also develop from pressure from family members and friends who believe that a man should be married.

Identifying Men Who Are Externally Motivated

Externally motivated men see the value of marriage through the eyes of others. They speak about marriage from a second-person point-of-view. Identifying externally motivated men is critical because you do not want to end up with a man who married you because he felt pressured or was strongly influenced by others. Make sure that your partner is not a praise-seeker. Here are some typical psychological and behavioral characteristics of externally motivated men:

1. Likes to please people, especially individuals who are close to them or have influence over them.

2. Lacks internal enthusiasm and motivation.

3. Engages in behavior that others think is best for them.

4. Has difficulty saying no or speaking up when under pressure from others.

5. Looks forward to receiving praise and awards for their decisions or behavior.

If you determine that your partner is planning to marry you because he is externally motivated, think twice. He might disapprove of serious relationships or marriage but will enter into marriage because he desires to have you cater to his needs. Also, be mindful that externally motivated men are more likely to select women based on their physical attributes or status, rather than their personalities.

Internal Motivation

Internal motivation is based on a man's self-reflective understanding that he has conquered his fear and he is ready to love you. He has made a decision to be emotionally available and is willing to give his all. Internal motivation comes from a man's personal drive and self-growth. His decision to marry you is influenced by his desire to achieve self-actualization. He understands that committing to you is the right thing to do and is driven internally to do so. An internally motivated man will commit to you because he enjoys what commitment means and offers. He does not look for external praise or awards.

Identifying Men Who Are Internally Motivated

Internally motivated men see the value of relationships through their own eyes. They speak about relationships from a personal point-of-view. Identifying internally motivated men is critical because you want to end up in a relationship with a man who married you because he felt personal enjoyment from being with you. Here are some typical psychological and behavioral characteristics of internally motivated men:

1. Listens to those who are close to him, but makes decisions based on personal fulfillment and needs.

2. Thrives on internal enthusiasm and motivation.

3. Engages in behavior that they feel is best for them.

4. Does not struggle with saying no or speaking up when under pressure from others.

5. Does not need praise or awards to feel good about their decisions or behavior.

You want to invest time in men who are internally motivated. They are the kind of guys who will enter into serious relationships or marriage because they see the value in doing so and are driven from within. Also, internally motivated men are more likely to select women based on their personalities and intrinsic motivation, rather than their physical attributes or status.

Exploring the two sources of motivation is very important when trying to determine if you should invest in a man. Understanding motivation is vital because it provides information about why men behave the way we do. By understanding a man's motivational source you can gain insight into how he will likely achieve or accomplish his goal to enter into marriage.

Motivation serves as a man's incentive to act or react in a certain manner. If you are interested in being with a man who will give his all in a relationship regardless of whether he is being praised or pressured from others, then you definitely want to invest in a man who is internally motivated. As mentioned previously, you want to avoid men who are only interested in being married to you because they like to receive praise or feel pressured. This group of men is difficult to interact with and I would advise you not to invest —exit immediately because you will not be able to sustain their attention.

Chapter 13

Find a Licensed Relationship Counselor: Help Thy Partner

Genesis 2:18, "And the LORD GOD said, 'It is not good that the man should be alone; I will make him an help meet for him.'

One of the primary reasons why so many women are single is because they have defective views about relationships. Many enter into relationships with a, "What can I get out of this" attitude. Instead of embracing the role of a helpmate, many women find fault in their partners and look to prosecute them. Ladies, if you are finding fault with your partner that means he needs your help. Use your gifts, skills and abilities that God blessed you with for the betterment of your relationship. By helping your partner, you ultimately help yourself.

From my observations, I have found that women who understand their role as a helpmate are more likely to fight for and keep their marriage intact when experiencing fear or emotional distress associated with relationship difficulty. In contrast, women who do not understand their role as a helpmate are more likely to flee when experiencing fear or emotional distress associated with relationship difficulty. Ninety percent of the marital therapy inquiries that I receive are initiated by God-loving women who have a desire to help mold and shape their partner into the man God wants him to be.

The helper role that women play is vital in fulfilling God's Divine plan for man and woman to live in harmony. This is because men typically do not feel comfortable seeking help and often minimize the role that fear or emotional distress play into their relationship difficulty. I point this out because you need to understand that God made you to be a helper. If your partner is struggling with fear regarding marriage and is willing to seek professional help you should provide assistance. Helping the man that you are with now might help you get what you deserve—lifetime commitment.

I encourage women to help and support their men by finding and attending professional pre-marital counseling because I believe that men should not be punished or abandoned due to experiencing fear or emotional distress if they are willing to receive help.

On your quest to secure lifetime commitment, you should strive to find a professional pre-marital counselor who is right for you and your partner. I strongly encourage you to attend pre-marital therapy, but take your time with finding the right counselor. Investing in a lifetime partner is a life-changing event, therefore it is essential that you find and work with a counselor who has some kind of professional training and/or formal education. Choosing the right counselor is a big decision. Factors to consider include their reputation, years of experience, credentials and ability to understand and meet your needs.

The ability to succeed in marriage does not occur without some form of professional counseling or guidance. Even the most nurturing, self-driven and productive women require guidance and seek advice from time to time. Based on the fact that relationships can be stressful at times, it is imperative to seek help when warranted. Women and men who have healthy marriages do not solely rely on their own knowledge as the gold template, but also seek knowledge from others as they endeavor to sustain healthy and productive marriages.

Here are three benefits of attending professional pre-marital counseling:

Benefit # 1: You can gain a better understanding of your partner's fear or emotional distress prior to making the ultimate investment.

Psychotherapists, such as myself, are skilled at assessing and treating men who suffer from fear or emotional distress associated with marital commitment. If you would like to do right by your partner and yourself, you should learn about human behavior and development from a professional. Seeking counseling can eliminate the need to play mind games with an unpredictable or emotionally distraught partner. Can you imagine what your relationship with your partner would be like if you secured proper knowledge and combined it with your love?

By attending professional counseling you can help your partner develop a plan for coping with his fear or distress. Through education and training, you can be taught to validate how your partner feels, learn to communicate effectively with him, and find out how to help him apply fear-reducing techniques such as Systematic Desensitization and Flooding.

Benefit # 2: If you decide to make the ultimate investment in your partner, you can learn to be more empathetic toward him.

By attending professional pre-marital counseling you can learn how to be more empathetic toward your partner. Learning to be empathetic is very important because most men's fear or emotional distress is associated with lack of trust in women or their inability to cope with vulnerable emotions. You can help your partner cope with his fear or emotional distress by being empathetic. As you model empathy, you can help your partner identify and process his fear in a healthy manner.

The most effective method for understanding men's behavior and minimizing fear is to establish empathetic relationships where they feel emotionally safe. Empathy is one of the most important interpersonal skills you can help your partner learn. Men who learn and apply empathy are more likely to be open-minded and transparent. Creating such a relationship with men can be challenging at times, especially when you are frustrated or feel discouraged. Demonstrating empathy toward a man who is emotionally detached and cold can be tough. Occasionally, you might feel like you are wasting your time; however, you must remember that failure to demonstrate empathy toward your man can cause him to believe that you do not have his best interest at heart. ***Translation****: He will not trust you.*

For most men, the desire to be respected, valued, and supported strongly influences how we behave. Therefore, your primary goal as a woman is to help your partner feel safe enough to discuss and express his fear or emotional distress with you. As you strive to become an empathetic support system for your partner, I am confident that you will develop a stronger emotional connection with him.

Benefit # 3: Learn what love is and be empowered to distinguish between lust and love before you invest.

Comprehending the essence and function of love can help you determine if you should enter into marriage, as well as help you determine if your relationship is built on and sustained on a solid foundation. Relationships that are based on love are more likely to last as compared to relationships that are developed out of a strong physical attraction, or lust. Many individuals build relationships out of lust because they do not understand what real love is. An issue that continues to astonish me daily is the belief that individuals are capable of developing and sustaining a relationship built on physical intimacy.

Some women and men have confused love with lust without realizing that they operate in opposition to each other. Love is associated with internal attributes (personality, values, the condition of a person's heart, etc.) and lust is associated with physical attributes (nice face, nice butt, sex appeal, etc.). Love requires you to be in a person's presence in order to develop feelings. Lust requires nothing more than a lustful eye. Love develops emotional intimacy while lust develops physical intimacy that is often mistaken for emotional intimacy. Many individuals build relationships out of lust because they do not understand what love is.

Understanding what love is and how it functions will greatly enhance your marriage investment skills. One cannot remove lust or any other vice from his or her life unless he or she understands what love is. We are living in times when more emphasis is placed on physical qualities and less on internal qualities. This trend is especially dangerous for single women who define the quality of their relationship based on superficial connections.

"Friends with benefits" relationships are typically lustful in nature and cripples single women's ability to establish relationships based on true love. You and your partner should explore the foundation in which your relationship was built on. A counselor can help you work through relationship challenges and develop insight into how to move forward in a healthy manner.

Attending professional pre-marital counseling is important and can prove to be beneficial to you and your partner. Do not continue to struggle unnecessarily. You should consistently try to learn as much as you can about your partner and develop a better understanding of what is needed to have a healthier relationship with him. This means that you should use all available resources.

By attending professional pre-marital counseling you will significantly enhance your ability to understand, influence and connect with your partner. Your dedication and commitment to obtaining knowledge will pay off if you decide to invest in him permanently. In the end, your relationship with your partner will flourish and an abundance of happiness and harmony will follow. I do not believe that a woman should walk away from her man if he has potential and is willing to grow. We all have shortcomings and should be supported if we are making genuine efforts to improve. Walking away should only happen, in my opinion, when a man refuses to help himself.

As stated previously, you cannot help or support someone who does not want to be helped or supported. It is important to be mindful of the fact that a man will not change unless he wants to do so. So do not think that you can change a man who does not want or desire help. You can help and support your partner and ask him to attend professional pre-marital counseling, but if he refuses, then what? Do not invest!

I said it before and I will say it one more time - *You Deserve More*! Know and believe this, and do not settle for less. Selecting and investing in a lifetime partner is actually pretty simple. All you have to do is apply what you have learned from reading this book, become a Proverbs 31 woman and "Trust in the LORD with all your heart; and lean not on your own understanding. In all your ways acknowledge Him, and He shall direct your paths," (Proverbs 3:5-6).

Chapter 14

R.E.A.L. TALK with Dr. Dwayne: Questions and Answers about Men and Relationships

On a yearly basis, I provide individual therapy and consultation services to hundreds of single women from different regions and cities around the world. Their backgrounds and experiences are very different in many ways and their views about men and relationships vary significantly. However, I am asked some of the same questions about men and relationships over and over again.

As I provide guidance and knowledge to women, I encourage them to keep it R.E.A.L. as they attempt to understand men and strive to successfully navigate through life, love and relationships. Please allow me to enlighten you about the structure of our R.E.A.L. Talk conversations.

R.E.A.L. Talk provides a road map for increasing women's self-awareness, self-determination and personal accountability in life, love and relationships.

R.E.A.L. is articulated as:

R- Realistic Approach

The "R" encourages you to approach situations in a **Realistic** manner. It is important to express an awareness of things as they really are and to use sound judgment and demonstrate empathy. Also seek to understand the source of problems before you attempt to address or solve them.

E – Rational Expectations

The "E" encourages you to exercise sound reasoning in order to develop rational **Expectations**. The expectations you have of yourself, others and life in general often reflect how you live your life. Eliminate irrational expectations and replace them with rational ones.

A – Positive Attitude

The "A" encourages you to maintain a positive **Attitude** of yourself and others. Do not let your attitude or feelings prevent you from being happy or progressing in life. Negativity begets negativity. Change starts with you.

L – Unconditional Love

The "L" encourages you to develop unconditional **Love** for yourself and others. Establish a deep, tender, indefinable feeling of affection and attentiveness toward yourself and others that is not determined or influenced by someone or something else.

I developed and used this powerful concept to conquer adversity in my life and I am dedicated to helping you do the same. I can help you apply this concept successfully in your life. I am standing by to help you expand your horizons by keeping it R.E.A.L.!

Questions and Answers about Men and Relationships

1. Are all single men damaged emotionally and should I avoid them at all cost?

No, all single men are not emotionally damaged. In my opinion emotionally-damaged men are very vindictive in nature and have intense hatred for women. Emotionally-damaged men are more likely to fight dirty and will do things to intentionally hurt you. A lot of single men who have trust issues occasionally check out emotionally and are somewhat selfish, but I do not consider them to be emotionally damaged. You should avoid single men who solely blame women for their heart pain. Accountability is important.

185

2. Are all single good men arrogant, selfish and overly confident?

No, I socialize with a number of single good men who are humble, down-to-earth, have nice jobs and are looking for women who can complement them. Their decision to be selective does not always equate to arrogance and selfishness. It is not wrong for a man to desire to be with a woman who complements him. Confident men typically do not do well in relationships with women who have self-esteem issues. No man wants to consistently give a woman compliments if she does not believe them. Compatibility is critical and should be present on several levels—spiritually, emotionally and behaviorally.

3. Are all single good men superficial?

No more than you are. In some form or fashion we are all superficial. How many times have you decided not to talk to a man because of his initial conversation, income, height, weight, clothing, shoes or overall physical appearance? Men and women typically see first and act second. We do not usually take the time to get to know members of the opposite sex if they are not appealing to the eye first. Like you, most men are wired to focus on things that really do not matter.

4. Why do men place conditions on how they love?

Most single men place conditions on how they love in an effort to maintain control of themselves and their relationships. Men have a strong need to be in control. Being in control empowers us to master our destiny and minimize our risk of being vulnerable. Without displaying vulnerability, we avoid the risk of being hurt. Men are motivated by receiving love, but the fear of pain, suffering and disappointment intensifies our need to place conditions on how we love.

5. Does a man's background and upbringing impact his view of women and relationships?

Yes, definitely. As a young boy I did not understand the worth of a woman. I was not educated or informed. No man ever taught me to respect a woman or appreciate her. I grew up viewing women negatively. I thought all women were weak because they did things that nobody else would do and supported men who did not support them or stay with them. My mother birthed eight children and practically raised us by herself. I remember having mixed feelings about my mother as a young child. I loved her wholeheartedly for taking care of me, but I was also angry with her. I never expressed my emotions or concerns to my mother, and as a result, I never understood her.

At a young age I held a negative view of women, especially black women. Witnessing the hardships and pain of my four sisters also compounded my ambivalence and negativity. They had children at early ages and engaged in activities similar to those of my mother: up-and-down relationships and raising their children alone. Only one of my sisters married, but this did not last long. Growing up and observing the hardships experienced by the women I cherished and loved was emotionally devastating. However, due to a lack of knowledge and respectful male role models, I grew up treating women the same way I saw men treating my mother and sisters (I explain how I dealt with this in my book: *"A Black Woman's Worth: My Queen and Backbone"*).

6. How important is it to share similar core values with a man?

It is extremely important to share similar core values with a man. Similarities set the stage for intimate relationships to develop. Individuals who appear to share similar interests and beliefs are more likely to enter into an intimate relationship. However, dissimilarity in core values will cause conflict. I have provided counseling to hundreds of couples who were troubled because they did not share similar core values about communication, money-management, expression of emotions and other issues that affect the quality of relationships. Interpersonal similarities are needed to develop a relationship, but similar core values are needed to sustain it. Value differences are either unrecognized or ignored in the beginning of most relationships because individuals believe that value differences should not be problematic for individuals who are deeply in love. Well, these differences can be problematic.

Make sure that your core values are compatible with any man that interests you. No other social institution is affected by the lack of similarities in core values like the institution of marriage. The best marriages have two individuals who are dedicated to working and developing similar core values—integrity, honesty, trust and mutual respect.

7. Why do men play games in relationships?

If a man feels that he cannot be himself in a relationship, he will send a representative who is flawless. However, if he feels that he can be himself, he will not send a representative, but will show up with his flaws visible. Men play games sometimes because we do not trust that you will accept us as is. There is a lot of pressure on men and some of us simply do not know how to handle the pressure. Game-playing can be costly both financially and emotionally and definitely ruins relationships. You can alleviate some of the game playing by being honest, respectful and accepting of a man's shortcomings.

8. How can I help restore a man's trust in women, especially in me?

Demonstrate compassion and do not judge him. Be consistent in your words and behavior because trust is earned over time and through action. If he feels that you have compassion for him, he is more likely to demonstrate compassion for you. If he truly believes that you have his best interest at hand and will not intentionally hurt him, he will be more likely to allow himself to fall in love, thus giving up the ability to control his heart.

9. How can a man hurt me if he loves me?

You must realize that love in and of itself is not enough to prevent a man from hurting you. Human beings were created out of love to love, but we allow our emotions to distort that love. I suggest that you look at the intent of a man's heart. I have learned that good-hearted men say and do bad things when their feelings are hurt. As a result, you should try to pay close attention to a man's underlying motives. If you detect that he is hurting you because he lacks insight as to how to express his emotions appropriately, provide support, guidance and pray. Basically, you should stick with him. If you detect that he is deliberately hurting you to be spiteful, you should seek professional help if warranted, provide support, guidance and also pray. If the deliberate behavior continues, you should simply remove yourself from the relationship.

10. If I love a man enough can (and will) he change?

Love without work does not last. I believe in the power of love, but I also believe in the power of work. You can love a man until you are blue in the face, but if he is not willing to or has no desire to change, he will not. Love is an emotion that influences the heart, not controls it. Men will

Dwayne L. Buckingham, Ph.D., LCSW, BCD

and can change if we want to and showing love to us can help move the process along.

11. Where do men learn how to love?

Our first example of how to show and express love in relationships comes from family interactions. Through direct involvement or observation we learn certain skills and habits, including how to love. Most men think we love the way we do based on our personal experiences alone, but this is not true. We have all been impacted by family experiences in some form or fashion. The processing of learning how to love is strongly influenced by the adults who raise us.

12. Do men get offended when women inquire about their income or money-making potential?

Yes! I can't tell you the number of times I have interacted with women who have placed more emphasize on my money-making potential than on my personal qualities. Men understand that personality does not pay bills, but we also understand that money and status cannot ensure or buy love. Take the time to get to know us before you size us up financially. We understand that we have to provide for you, but we also want to feel like you are invested in us, not our wallets.

13. Does setting or establishing standards really work?

Yes and no. You can establish all kinds of standards, but a man will not change unless he wants to. Many of you get advice that suggests you should do this and you should do that to entrap or keep your man. Take heed, it does not matter what you do. For every behavior that you engage in to entrap a man, he has an escape plan. Remember, I told you that men are skilled at psychological warfare. You can try to think like a man, but it will not and does not work. As a matter of fact, you should think like a woman and act like one. Quit playing games. Healthy relationships are built on effective and honest communication, self-reflection and self-growth. If you have to play mind games with a man by thinking like him, then you should not be with him.

14. How can I tell if a man is insecure or secure about being in a relationship?

This may be challenging for you, but it is fairly easy to spot insecure men. One effective way to find out if a man is insecure is to pay attention to how emotionally aroused he becomes when he speaks about commitment and relationships. If a man speaks about commitment and relationships with excitement, openness, optimism and eagerness, he is probably secure in his identity. However, if a man speaks about commitment and relationships with boredom, caution, pessimism and apathy, he is probably insecure.

15. Do emotionally unavailable men care about women?

Yes, they do care about women, but they care about themselves more. At the end of the day, when a man chooses to interact with and lead you on, regardless of the understanding you all have, he is being selfish, especially if he knows that you want more. Caring means letting go!

16. Are men stronger than women?

Most women and men would agree that men are typically stronger than women from a physical standpoint; however, when dealing with emotions that is a different story. When women get hurt you are likely to mourn for a short period and move on after actively coping with your pain. Men, on the other hand, will often allow heartbreak and trauma to fester and lead to emotional roadblocks that hinder our ability to move on.

17. Do single men avoid marriage and commitment because they are afraid of taking on more responsibility?

Some do and some don't. I believe that a large percentage of men do not mind the responsibility that comes along with being the head of a household because we expect to do that. Most men are afraid to rely on women for emotional support and comfort. Also, single men take pride in and are used to being self-reliant.

18. How can I tell if a man lusts after me or loves me?

Unfortunately, women and men have confused lust with love without realizing that they operate in opposition to each other. If a man truly loves you he will wait to be married before having sex, if that is what you desire; if he lusts after you he will pressure you to jump in bed before marriage. If a man loves you, he will appreciate your mind; if he lusts after you he will appreciate your body (I explain the difference between love and lust in my book, *Unconditional Love: What Every Woman and Man Desires in a Relationship*).

19. What are the chances of a man marrying in his late thirties?

Not good. Most men who are really serious about marriage typically find a wife before they hit thirty. Men who are 35-years-old and older are more likely to remain single, although they might express a desire to get married. Nothing is etched in stone, but research shows that men who are 35 and older typically do not marry.

20. Can single men live pleasurable lifestyles alone?

"Pleasurable lifestyle" is a subjective term, but I believe so. I know a lot of single guys who live good lives and appear to be satisfied with their lifestyles. They find pleasure in accomplishing career goals, traveling and doing things they enjoy doing. In regard to having and wanting companionship, many of them are open to marriage, but do not feel a need to rush into it. I hate to say it, but companionship can be bought. A man who is not looking for a serious relationship is okay with spending money on women for personal gain.

21. Can single men refrain from having sex for extended periods?

Yes, I am a living example. I practiced abstinence for 5 years. And believe me I am not gay and nothing is medically wrong with me. Some men do grow up and start using our big head more than we use our little head. I took some time to get myself together. After years of going through drama, I decided to stop having sex with women. This was not easy, but I learned a lot about myself and women after I stopped sleeping around. I learned to be disciplined and learned that women who respect their bodies cannot give themselves without wanting more. I refrained by not putting myself in risky situations—no opportunity, no sex. Thank God that it paid off because I am happily married now.

22. This guy keeps telling me that he loves me, but is not in love with me. What does that mean?

Over the past fourteen years, I have heard hundreds of men tell women they love them, but are not in love with them. I started to inquire about the meaning and kept notes. After reviewing my notes and discussing this with men, I came up with the following explanation: when a man tells a woman he loves her, he means that he cares about her deeply and would never want anything to happen to her. He views her as someone who is special. He distinguishes love from being in love by detaching emotionally. When he says that he is not in love, he is saying that he does not feel attached to you on an emotional level—he does not feel spiritually or intimately attached.

23. Do men like women with masculine tendencies?

No! Being independent and successful is totally different from being masculine. Most men don't want a woman who acts just as aggressively as he does. I know this does not sound fair, but many men are attracted to and want a woman who is feminine on many levels. The quickest way to turn a man off is to start acting tough and insensitive. I often encourage women not to let men take them outside of their feminine zone—the place where you feel most comfortable.

24. Why do some women choose to date or get involved with emotionally unavailable men?

I have found that women who lack understanding of their worth typically get involved with emotionally unavailable men. Most of them suffer from low self-esteem.

On the other hand, desperation can play a major role. I have worked with some very confident and strong women who have found themselves in these kinds of relationships because they felt that their options were limited—struggling with the "a good man is hard to find" issue.

25. What can a woman do to break off a fling or relationship with an emotionally unavailable man?

Stop spending time with him. Minimize and eventually cut off all contact. I would suggest that you do this slowly so that you do not experience intense emotional withdrawal. If you pull back too soon the withdrawal might be too much for you to handle and you will keep going back. Develop a withdrawal plan or contact me.

26. Should I give into dating men who do not meet my standards?

No, please stick to your standards. I say this because it is not fair to you or the man if you lower your standards. Settling is never good because you will always have a yearning for what you think you are missing. If you like a man with a certain build, look or intellect you should date men who meet your criteria. Be careful when dating men who do not meet your criteria. Love will and can creep up on you and before you know it you are in a relationship and unhappy. However, if you end up in a relationship with a man who does not meet all of your standards, learn to love him unconditionally and keep your hands and eyes off other men.

27. Is rebound love and dating bad for me?

Yes! Some of your girlfriends might tell you that the easiest way to get over a man is to get with another one. This is bad advice. Please allow your heart to heal so that you do not enter into another relationship with unresolved emotional baggage. Also, if you move too quickly, you might end up in another bad relationship. Remember that good things come to those who wait, and heal properly.

28. I am not good at identifying men who do not have my best interest at hand. How can I improve in this area?

Contact me!

29. Should I date casually so I can get better at screening men?

Some people say that practice makes perfect, but it depends on what you mean by casual dating. In this day and age, men and women view dating differently. If you decide to engage in this behavior, I highly recommend that you make it clear what your intentions are. This could be helpful if you have not ventured onto the dating scene much. By meeting different men you can get an idea of what you like and do not like. Be careful though because you can get caught up. You might find that you like some qualities in one man and some qualities in another man.

30. Do married women suffer more than single women when relationships do not work out?

Not necessarily. What most people fail to realize is that a piece of paper does not determine how a person feels about or copes with heartbreak, love or commitment. I have provided counseling to thousands of single women and men who have experienced just as much pain and distress in their relationships as married women. The difference is not emotional in nature, but legal. Married women often feel trapped when things do not work out, but so do single women who have children and other obligations with their counterparts.

31. What will increase my chances of entering into a healthy relationship with a man?

Acquiring knowledge and seeking professional guidance are key to having healthy relationships, so please do not depend on your experience alone. Vernon Law, a famous baseball player, once stated, "Experience is a hard teacher because she gives the test first and the lesson afterwards." Instead of feeling frustrated and discouraged on a daily basis, try equipping yourself with proper knowledge so that you can be adequately prepared for the test—dealing with an unpredictable man.

It is unfortunate that one of the most important aspects of life—developing healthy relationships—is a task that many women believe can best be accomplished through experimentation and practice. In others areas of your life, where you are responsible for others, you are required to study and acquire knowledge before you can perform those tasks. For example, before you can secure your driver's license, you must study the examination book and pass the test. This process was put into place and is enforced to ensure that you do not harm yourself or others when you get on the byways and highways. Why is there no process or plan in place that requires women and men to secure knowledge before entering into relationships?

32. Do women check out emotionally? If yes, how is their emotional unavailability different from men's?

Yes! I have met plenty of women who are emotionally unavailable for various reasons (busy, focused on career, rebounding from a painful relationship, etc.) just like men. However, women who are truly interested in having companionship tend to rebound more quickly than men. This happens particularly because women are emotional creatures. Also, women are more resilient than men when it comes to their emotions.

33. Why do so many smart women like me fall in love or develop interest in men who do not truly care about us?

Unlike men, you allow your emotions to guide you. You accept emotions and release them. Men on the other hand, have been raised to hide and repress emotions. Falling in love is an emotional process for most women, but many men make it a logical process. Contrary to popular belief, emotions control your thinking and behavior, not intellect.

Work to neutralize your emotional intensity and you will be capable of making more rational decisions about men.

34. Do men process and make decisions differently than we do?

Men and women process in similar manners, but make decisions differently. Both women and men process in the following manner: Think-Feel-Do. However, men typically make decisions based on what we think, and women typically make decisions based on how you feel.

35. Is it healthy for men to avoid or repress their emotions?

No. A lot of men continue to have problems in their relationships because we do not know how to deal with emotions. Emotional stagnation is a major problem for men. Men who fail to deal with emotions will often drain the energy of those around them. Given this, do not enter into a relationship with a man who has no desire to improve his emotional well-being. Remember: having qualifications does not mean qualified.

36. Do men feel secure and confident when they are in positions to provide for their families?

Yes and no. You are led to believe that a man will feel secure and confident once he is in a position to take care of you—this is partially true. The whole truth is this: a man's sense of security stems from his ability to address and protect his emotional well-being first and yours second. If a man feels or believes that you will or have the potential to hurt him emotionally, he will not put you first in his life. Losing money and material items hurts men, but not like heartbreak does. Being able to provide for and protect you is one thing, but he will only do that if he feels safe and secure with himself.

37. One of my love languages is attention, but I am not getting any in my relationship. Should I leave my boyfriend?

Understanding and knowing what you need in a relationship is very important. The need for respect and attention are very basic needs, but are essential for building a healthy marriage. Women should be thinking about their partners' behavior prior to agreeing to marriage. Commitment, consideration and communication are very important and you should not commit to a partner who appears to be struggling with all three. Take some time to work through your relationship issues and hold your partner accountable before moving forward.

38. My trust in my partner is shattered. What can I tell him to help him regain my trust?

Listed below are a few strategies that you can share to restore your trust in your partner and get your relationship back:

1. Tell him to be truthful moving forward and take responsibility for his actions. Lying about the simplest thing can create additional suspicion and set you back significantly. Encourage him to communicate. No matter how he feels it is important to communicate in an open and honest manner. Tell him to mean what he says and follow through with action. Lying is not an option.

2. Ask him to commit to change. He has to be willing to do whatever it takes to modify the behavior that created the mistrust. If he has been devoted to himself, change should occur immediately. Remind him that devotion to himself will cause him to be by himself.

3. Share openly. Ask him to give you access to his cell phone, social media accounts and email contacts. This might be difficult to do, but if he desires to restore trust and save the relationship he will not allow his self-righteous need for privacy to override your need for trust and love. He can make a short-term sacrifice for a long-term benefit. Privacy is important, but so is trust.

4. Ask him to reexamine his values and personal needs. If he values the relationship then he needs to spend more time learning how to make it work. He needs to be aware of and work through selfish and self-centered thinking. If he finds himself focusing on his personal needs without considering your needs, you are in a bad place. Some people love the idea of marriage, but not the personal and interpersonal work that comes with it.

5. Tell him to eliminate fear of living without you. Fear of living without someone is not a good reason to stay in a relationship. True happiness occurs when you enjoy living with them. He should allow love to guide his actions and fear.

By applying the 5 strategies listed above, your partner will be better positioned to regain your trust. Think positive, remain calm and be honest as you move forward on your journey.

39. How do you know when you should quit and move on?

You should call it quits when your significant other stops striving for excellence in life and love. Striving is the key to thriving. You cannot get excellent without effort. There are no perfect matches or love. Like anything else in life, love is expressed differently and shifts based on circumstances. However, as long as individuals are striving and giving 100% to achieve personal and relational prosperity, I believe that you should not throw in the towel. Be realistic and prepare to work in order to develop and sustain a healthy relationship. If he is willing to do the work to achieve excellence in life and love, give him a chance, but if he is not willing to devote the time and energy to work at it—*call it quits and move on!* Do not cheat yourself and understand that you deserve better. "He who finds a wife, finds a good thing, and obtains favor from the Lord" (Proverbs 18:22).

40. What makes marriage work?

Marriage works well when individuals feel respected and are functioning as teammates. Teammates work together to achieve a common goal. Each member of the team is respected for what he or she brings to the table. Life and relationship decisions are made jointly and each person feels valued. Teammate thinking is what makes marriage work.

Epilogue:
Shallowness Creates
Problems for Women

I cannot emphasize to you enough the importance of looking beyond a man's surface. By focusing primarily on a man's qualifications, physical appearance, and ability to provide and protect, you will never understand men or find true love.

Do not believe the hype about men being simple. Yes, we have some very basic needs, but nothing is simple when it comes to meeting them. Be careful of the words you choose to use when you describe and interact with men—no man likes to be referred to as simple. This is very important for you to undestand because if you view men as being simple, you will treat us in a simple manner. And I can promise you that this will not turn out well for you. As I mentioned in the introduction, you should be very selective about the information you choose to receive and use. We are all guilty of making generalizations, but remember that every man is unique in his own right. Some men are more complex than others.

In conclusion, I ask that you dig a little deeper and keep the following quote in mind as you select and invest in your lifetime partner.

> *When you meet a man, you judge him by*
> *his clothes; when you leave, you judge*
> *him by his heart.*

— Russian Proverb

Food for Thought:
Quotes about Love, Women and Men

Love

---

*Love is not a feeling. Love is an action,
an activity. ... Genuine love implies
commitment and the exercise of wisdom.
... Love is the will to extend oneself for
the purpose of nurturing one's own or
another's spiritual growth. ... True love
is an act of will that often transcends
ephemeral feelings of love or cathexis, it
is correct to say, "Love is as love does."*

– Scott Peck

*Love is when you look into someone's
eyes and see their heart.*

– Jill Petty

*A man falls in love through his eyes, a
woman through her ears.*

– Woodrow Wyatt

I don't want to live—I want to love first,
and live incidentally.

— Zelda Fitzgerald

You know it's love when you want to give
joy and damn the consequences."

— Frank Herbert

Do you love me because I am beautiful,
or am I beautiful because you love me?

— Cinderella

Love doesn't make the world go round.
Love is what makes the ride worthwhile.

— Franklin P. Jones

Love is an ocean of emotions entirely
surrounded by expenses.

— Lord Dewar

Love is being stupid together.

— Paul Valery

You never lose by loving. You always
lose by holding back.

— Barbara De Angelis

Love is life. And if you miss love, you miss life.

– Leo Buscaglia

Love has its own time, its own season, and its own reasons from coming and going. You cannot bribe it or coerce it or reason it into staying. You can only embrace it when it arrives and give it away when it comes to you.

– Kent Nerburn

Love enables you to put your deepest feelings and fears in the palm of your partner's hand, knowing they will be handled with care.

– Carl S. Avery

Love is patient, love is kind.

It does not envy, it does not boast, it is not proud.

It is not rude, it is not self-seeking.

It is not easily angered, it keeps no record of wrongs.

Love does not delight in evil, but rejoices with the truth.

It always protects, always trusts, always hopes, always perseveres.

Love never fails.

– Corinthians 13:4-8

---

*A woman in love can't be reasonable—or
she probably wouldn't be in love.*

– Mae West

*There are no good girls gone wrong—
just bad girls found out.*

– Mae West

*Good girls go to heaven, bad girls go
everywhere.*

– Mae West

*Women always worry about things that
men forget; men always worry about
things women remember.*

– Majorie Kinnan Rawlings

*Women have wonderful instinct about
things. They can discover everything
except the obvious.*

– Oscar Wilde

*Women marry men hoping they will
change. Men marry women hoping they
will not. So each is inevitably
disappointed.*

– Albert Einstein

Men are anxious to improve their circumstances, but are unwilling to improve themselves; they therefore remain bound.

– James Allen

Men are what their mothers made them.

– Ralph Waldo Emerson

Men are rich only as they give. He who gives great service gets great rewards.

– Elbert Hubbard

A man is already halfway in love with any woman who listens to him.

– Brendan Francis

Men are all alike .... except the one you've met who is different.

– Mae West

A man is not where he lives, but where he loves.

– Latin Proverb

I would rather trust a woman's instinct than a man's reason.

– Stanley Baldwin

An archaeologist is the best husband a woman can have. The older she gets the more interested he is in her.

– Agatha Christie

I love the man that can smile in trouble, that can gather strength from distress, grow by reflection.

– Thomas Paine

Understanding Abuse

It is important to understand abuse. Some of you are in abusive relationships and do not know it. Love should not hurt, at least not intentionally. I hope you find this information to be helpful.

Different Forms of Abuse

- Physical Abuse (inflicting physical discomfort, pain or injury); Slapping, hitting, burning, punching, restraining, sexually assaulting, handling roughly, etc.

- Sexual Abuse (forced sexual contact, rape or incest)

- Psychological/emotional abuse (diminishing your identity and self-worth); Threatening, insulting, name--calling, yelling, imitating, ignoring, isolating, etc.

- Neglect (failure to meet your needs or those of others); Inadequate physical or emotional care: denial of food, water, clothing, health care, etc.

Symptoms of Abuse — "Misuse of Power and Control"

Using Physical Abuse
- Pushed or shoved you
- Held you to keep you from leaving

219

- Slapped or bit you
- Kicked, choked, hit or punched you
- Locked you out of the house
- Abandoned you in a dangerous place
- Refused to help you when you were sick, injured or pregnant
- Subjected you to reckless driving
- Forced you off the road or kept you from driving
- Raped you
- Threatened or hurt you with a weapon

Using Sexual Abuse

- Told anti-woman jokes or made demeaning remarks about women
- Insisted that you dress in a more sexual way than you wanted
- Called you derogatory sexual names like "whore" or "freak"
- Forced you to strip when you did not want to
- Forced you to have unwanted sex with others or forced you to watch others
- Forced sex after beatings
- Forced sex for the purpose of hurting you with objects or weapons
- Committed sadistic sexual acts

Using Emotional Abuse

- Put you down
- Made you feel bad about yourself
- Called you names
- Made you think you are crazy
- Played mind games with you
- Humiliated you
- Made you feel guilty

Using Male Privilege

- Treated you like a servant
- Made all the big decisions
- Acted like the "master of the castle"
- Defined men's and women's roles

Using Economic Abuse

- Prevented you from getting or keeping a job
- Made you ask for money
- Gave you an allowance
- Took your money
- Didn't let you know about or have access to family income

Using Coercion and Threats

- Made or carried out threats to do something to hurt you
- Threatened to leave you, to commit suicide, to report you to welfare
- Made you drop charges
- Made you do illegal things

Using Intimidation

- Made you afraid by using looks, gestures, or actions
- Smashed things
- Abused pets
- Displayed weapons

Using Children

- Made you feel guilty about the children
- Used the children to relay messages
- Used visitation to harass you
- Threatened to take the children away

Using Isolation

- Controlled what you do, who you see and talk to, what you read and where you go
- Limited your outside involvement
- Used jealousy to justify actions

Minimizing, Denying, Blaming

- Made light of the abuse and did not take your concerns about it seriously
- Said the abuse didn't happen
- Shifted responsibility for abusive behavior
- Said you caused the abuse

Sweet Baby Syndromes (How He Gets to Come Back)

- Honeymoon Syndrome
- Super Dad Syndrome
- Revival Syndrome
- Sobriety Syndrome
- Counseling Syndrome

Common Characteristics of a Battered Woman

- Has low self-esteem
- Is a traditionalist about the home
- Accepts responsibility for the batterer's actions
- Suffers from guilt, yet denies terror and anger
- Has severe stress reactions with psychophysiological complaints
- Uses sex as a way to establish intimacy
- Believes that no one will be able to help her resolve her predicament

Common Characteristics of the Batterer

- Has low self-esteem
- Believes all the myths about battering relationships
- Is a traditionalist
- Blames others for his actions
- Is pathologically jealous
- Presents a dual personality
- Has severe stress reactions
- Uses sex as an act of aggression
- Does not believe violent behavior should have negative consequences

Reaction of Women Being Beaten

- Denial
- Blaming self
- Ambivalence

Long-Term Effects of Domestic Violence

- Physical
- Mental
- Economic
- Affects children

Abuse/Neglect Screening Questionnaire

If you answer yes to one or more of the questions below, please talk to someone you trust and/or seek help.

- Has any man ever touched you without your consent?
- Has any man ever made you do things you didn't want to do?

- Has any man taken anything that was yours without asking?
- Has any man ever scolded or threatened you?
- Are you afraid of your man?
- Are you alone much of the time?
- Do you have low self-esteem?
- Do you feel like you are emotionally unstable?
- Do you feel depressed? Are you anxious frequently? Are you angry often?
- Do you feel hopelessness? Do you feel guilty? Are you sad?
- Are you overly compliant or passive?
- Are you extremely aggressive or demanding?
- Are you extremely dependent on your man?

Seek help immediately if you or a friend is being abused. Battered Women's National Hotline: 1-800-799-7233
Abuse Hotline: 1-888-743-5754.

Scheduling for Seminars or Speaking Engagements

Expanding Horizons by Keeping it "R.E.A.L."

Dr. Buckingham conducts educational wellness seminars for individuals, families, groups, churches and organizations throughout the year.

"You Deserve More" is one of the most requested seminars; however, Dr. Dwayne conducts seminars on a variety of relationship and life topics.

RHCS is dedicated to helping you expand your

horizons!

To book an event:

R.E.A.L. Horizons Consulting Service, LLC
P.O. Box 2665
Silver Spring, MD 20915

240-242-4087 Voice Mail
www.realhorizonsdlb.com

I hope this book has been a blessing to you and I welcome your comments.

dwayne@realhorizonsdlb.com

This book can also be purchased online at:

www.realhorioznsdlb.com

Amazon.com

About the Author

Dr. Dwayne L. Buckingham, LCSW, BCD is President and Chief Executive Officer of R.E.A.L. Horizons Consulting Service, LLC. He is a highly acclaimed international clinical psychotherapist, relationship expert and corporate consultant. Over the past 17 years, he has dedicated his life to helping individuals, couples and corporate leaders build healthy relationships by providing world-class empathy and resiliency consulting. Dr. Buckingham is well respected among his professional colleagues and is known as "The Empathy and Resiliency Doctor or The E.R. Doctor."

As a commissioned officer in the United States Air Force for nearly a decade, Dr. Buckingham provided psychological assessments, treatment and psycho-educational training to over 30,000 individuals, couples, groups, and families worldwide. Currently, he works with wounded warriors and other personnel assigned to the Walter Reed National Military Medical Center in Bethesda, Maryland.

Dr. Buckingham is a highly sought-after motivational speaker, author, seminar facilitator, relationship expert and executive coach. He is also an active member of the National Association of Social Workers and Kappa Alpha Psi Fraternity, Inc.

A few of Dr. Buckingham's media appearances include: NBC, ABC, Fox, The CW 11, The Daily Drum and the Huffington Post. Please visit his website at www.realhorizonsdlb.com for more information.